FOR MY DEAR DAD, DAVID,
WHO, IN ALL HONESTY,
WOULD PROBABLY RATHER
GO FLY-FISHING THAN
HAVE A PARTY.

Alice Hart

FRIENDS AT MY TABLE

PHOTOGRAPHY BY EMMA LEE

ROOST
BOOKS

BOSTON

2013

FOOD, SETTING, AND NOSTALGIA ARE SO KEENLY INTERTWINED. Unsurprising, perhaps, when one
considers how the milestones peppering our lives are marked with celebrations
and gatherings. Keeping such merrymaking and a generous number of guests in
mind, this is a book of menus, recipes, and advice to assist when cooking for those
jolly occasions, be they humble, fanciful, or downright elaborate.

I can think of few more rewarding occupations than cooking a supper, lunch, or
brunch for a good crowd of loved ones. Moreover, I hope that within these pages you
will find techniques and tips to make life—and your enjoyment of the party—that
much easier.

We, the enthusiastic eaters and the cooks of today, have undeniably well-informed
tastes. This doesn't mean that the recipes we cook should be complicated. The most
important thing is always that the food be delicious, but if dishes can also be appealing
in color and contrasting in texture, you will be onto a winner. Using both the food and
the changing seasons to help create a warm atmosphere—a sense of occasion, if you
like—makes a party memorable without breaking the bank.

The recipes and menus in this book are balanced and well-suited to the unpredictable
game of party-throwing. Cooking for larger numbers might seem daunting but, really,
it needn't be. Last-minute frying, slicing, and dicing send me into a tailspin; instead,
I'll throw in every simple technique I know to prep in advance and get ahead, safe in
the knowledge that supper is in hand. It takes a certain adjustment to think in terms
of hearty, bountiful, and often family-style dishes, rather than anything fiddly or fussy.
These are intended to be happy, relaxed occasions, and what would be the point in
inviting friends over if you didn't get to put your tools down early, pick up a glass
of something fizzy, and enjoy yourself? List makers rejoice, for this is your time. A
simple battle strategy, some planning, and a few lists will help keep you on track.

From a small-but-chic country wedding to a bountiful New Year's Eve spread,
via spring brunch and weekends away with friends, the emphasis on seasonality
throughout these chapters is not just for show, it will also help to create a fitting
atmosphere. Embrace the whimsy each changing month of the year has to offer
and use it to your advantage. The message has truly hit home now: food in season
bursts with flavor. In addition, said bounty is nearly always cheaper and has a higher
nutritional value than its off-season relations, so take advantage of any gluts you find
at the markets. If you are making a recipe at a different time of year than originally
intended, substitute like-for-like vegetables or fruit—root for root, berry for berry—
and perhaps have a test run in advance; there are plenty of suggestions for alternative
ingredients in the recipe introductions.

Getting the best value from a joint of meat, a magnificent fish, or a crate of fruit is paramount, especially when shelling out larger quantities for a special occasion. Brining and smokily roasting, say, a hefty slab of bottom round to make a great quantity of spiced pastrami, as in the New Year chapter you'll find here, takes so much pressure off the cook as all the preparation happens in the preceding week. Shaving the pastrami into slices, to serve on rye bread with mustard, pickles, and winter salad greens, will stretch a handsome, yet thrifty, piece of beef a long way.

The best advice I can give you in all this is to keep a calm head. Try not to run yourself ragged or abandon a recipe simply because you can't locate a particular ingredient. Instead, make a logical and seasonal substitution. Similar herbs, cuts of meat, fish, and whole dairy are usually interchangeable, as long as you use a dash of common sense and don't stray too far from the original. Have faith in your taste buds though; if you can't find kaffir lime leaves, throw in some lime zest and don't give it another thought. You are in charge of this food and not the other way around!

I have catered for events, large and small, cheffed in bars and restaurants and private houses, run baking stalls, cooked hundreds and hundreds of recipes for glossy photo shoots, and written and developed even more for print. Two nuggets of wisdom I have gleaned are, first, to shop and prepare in advance—in fact, as far in advance as is humanly possible—and, second, to spread the workload out, rather than expecting to get everything done on the day. As I'll show you, many of the cunning techniques chefs employ when preparing food for large crowds prove incredibly useful to the home cook, but none as much as assembling a *mise en place*, where, if the entire dish can't be finished before the day, the ingredients are chopped or partially cooked ahead, ready to be put together to order. You will find few pyrotechnics in this book, no wildly difficult techniques or finicky sauces, but, as I point out in the relevant recipes, feeding ten, sixteen, or even twenty well requires forethought, and I can guide you through the process. I'm not suggesting for a minute that you cook in such volumes every day; I certainly don't. However, I'm used to, and relaxed about, cooking for large numbers. With the right recipes, cooking for ten rather than two can be just as easy, and you might as well make a real night of it.

There would be little point in a cookbook that isn't useful and usable to a broad range of readers, so a balance had to be found in the party sizes. There are menus for not-so-daunting groups of six, right up to menus for twenty, but, apart from a sumptuous strawberry and vanilla wedding cake to feed the five thousand, that was the point at which I stopped. Most recipes can be halved or quartered if needed, and, where suitable, I have tried to indicate this in the text. Don't be afraid to make a larger quantity, as written, and freeze the remainder for another time. You'll probably thank your kind and organized self in the future when you need an instant supper or dessert.

A real advantage of catering for large numbers is that the more people you have to feed, the less you have to make. What I mean is, there's a magical point at which the finished quantities seem to stretch themselves. You might expect, quite logically, that a recipe for four could be multiplied by four to serve sixteen . . . but no. In reality, there will be enough food for eighteen, perhaps even more. Recipe multiplication is a fickle beast, but at least it errs on the side of generosity, which is surely the key to a great party.

The twelve menus here, three for each season, have been carefully tested and balanced to suit the occasion, season, and party size, but if one look at them fills you with terror, have no shame at all in cherry-picking what you can cope with and simplifying or delegating the rest. Serve fresh fruit and bought ice cream for dessert; draft in help from friends and family; delegate an entire course to somebody else; serve a simple salad and some lovely bread with a main course, and leave it at that.

It takes a certain arrogance to assume that you will follow like a lamb and make everything on a suggested menu. Each recipe should stand proud and alone, so of course you are encouraged to cook each on its own, without accompanying dishes. Making a menu in its entirety, however, shouldn't cause any problems regarding the different timings, oven temperatures, and oven space called for. I often move some of the cooking outside, to take the pressure off the kitchen. Building your own firepit or hot smoker outdoors may not fall into the category of upright entertaining (a distinct plus, "entertaining" being a hateful word anyway), but it will make cooking that majestic joint of meat or clutch of root vegetables exciting and earthy, while including your friends in the process.

All this wining and dining goes beyond getting food on the table, and I hope you will glean some relevant, and decidedly nonStepford, ideas to help in pushing that boat out in a variety of settings. I would rarely bother to set tables rigidly, for example: flatware piled into jars and set on the table for people to help themselves looks charming and will save you considerable fuss. There is no rule saying chairs, crockery, and tables need to match or that seating arrangements can't be on the cozy side . . . so relax and have fun with it all.

Gathering friends and family together to eat, drink, and make merry need not feel like a test or an exercise in stress; the main aim is that everybody has a good time. Including you.

SEASONALITY CHART

When fruits, herbs, and vegetables are at their best, based on UK (and Northern Europe)

SPRING

ALPHONSO MANGO | ASPARAGUS
BROCCOLI | CAULIFLOWER | CELERY ROOT
CHICORY | CHIVES | CUCUMBER | DILL | LEEK
LETTUCES (*early*) | PARSLEY | PASSION FRUIT
PURPLE-SPROUTING BROCCOLI | RADISH | RHUBARB
SCALLION | SPINACH | STRAWBERRY (*early*)| TARRAGON

Summer

APRICOT | ARTICHOKE | ARUGULA | BASIL
BEET | BLACKBERRY | BLACK CURRANT
BLUEBERRY | BOK CHOY AND PAK CHOI
BROCCOLI | CARROT | CELERY | CHERRY | CHERVIL
CHILI | CHIVES | CILANTRO | CUCUMBER | DILL | EGGPLANT | FAVA
BEAN | FENNEL (*bulb*) | FIG | GARLIC | GOOSEBERRY | LETTUCES
(*summer*) | MELON | MINT | MULBERRY | NEW POTATO | ONION
AND SHALLOT | OREGANO | PARSLEY | PEA AND SUGAR SNAP PEA
PLUM | POTATO (*maincrop*) | RADISH | RASPBERRY | RED CURRANT
RHUBARB | ROSEMARY | SAGE | SCALLION | SNOW PEAS | SPINACH
STRAWBERRY | SWEET CORN | TARRAGON | THYME | TOMATO
TURNIP | WATERCRESS | WILD MUSHROOM | ZUCCHINI

FALL

APPLE | ARUGULA | BEET | BLACKBERRY
BUTTERNUT SQUASH | CARROT | CELERY
CELERY ROOT | CHICORY | CHIVES | FENNEL (*bulb*)
FIG | GARLIC | GRAPE | HAZELNUT | HORSERADISH
JERUSALEM ARTICHOKE | KALE | KOHLRABI | LEEK | LETTUCES (*late*)
NECTARINE | ONION AND SHALLOT | PARSLEY | PARSNIP | PEACH
PEAR | PEPPER | PINEAPPLE | PLUM | POTATO (*maincrop*) | PUMPKIN
RADISH | RASPBERRY | ROSEMARY | SAGE | SCALLION | SWEET
CORN | TARRAGON | THYME | TOMATO | WATERCRESS | WILD
MUSHROOM | WINTER SQUASH

WINTER

BEET | BLOOD ORANGE | CAULIFLOWER | CELERY
ROOT | CELERY | CHICORY | HORSERADISH
JERUSALEM ARTICHOKE | KALE | LEEK
LEMON | MANGO | ONION AND SHALLOT
ORANGE | PARSNIP | PASSION FRUIT | POMEGRANATE
POTATO (*maincrop*) | PUMPKIN | PURPLE-SPROUTING BROCCOLI
RADISH | RHUBARB | ROSEMARY | SAGE | SCALLION
THYME | TURNIP | WILD MUSHROOM | WINTER LETTUCES (*until
first frosts unless protected*) | WINTER SQUASH

EQUIPMENT AND TECHNIQUES:
Cooking for a Crowd

Food safety is something to bear in mind constantly when cooking for larger numbers. It is obviously paramount that food, especially meat, be cooked adequately, and it can be easier to miss when you have large quantities or multiples to deal with, or when using alternative and slow-cooking methods, such as smoking. I use a **MEAT THERMOMETER**, just to make sure. Stick it into the center of the meat and adhere to the following:

	VERY RARE–RARE	MEDIUM	WELL DONE
BEEF, LAMB, AND VENISON	113–122°F	140°F	158°F
PORK	N/A	158°F	167°F
POULTRY	N/A	N/A	180°F *(min. temp.)*
GAME BIRDS	N/A	165°F *(min. temp.)*	*above* 165°F

An **OVEN THERMOMETER** is also essential. Most ovens run hot or cool, or have hot spots; you might not even realize your oven is actually at a different temperature to that indicated on the dial. When you've spent more time and effort on larger quantities of ingredients, it would be especially heartbreaking to scorch them through no fault of your own, so buy an oven thermometer—they are reasonably priced and widely available in kitchen and grocery stores—and adhere to its temperature reading, rather than your oven dial.

It will involve spending money, but if you're really serious about getting some fast prep done, a **FOOD PROCESSOR** will help you out to no end. It's a somewhat contentious method (the purists would say always use your hands), but I use mine to make pie dough in batches.

It takes mere minutes and, if you are careful to use the pulse button and not overwork the flour, produces chilled, short results every time. Thicker slicing, rough chopping, batter mixing, sauces, and mayonnaise can all be churned out in a food processor with very little bother. I would highly recommend the KitchenAid make for their sturdiness and good looks. The same goes for their freestanding food mixer, but if you are watching the cents, a good compromise would be . . .

An **ELECTRIC HAND WHISK**—a heavy-duty model rather than something too cheap and flimsy—will do you great service for smoothly whipping up batters, meringues, cream, etc.

The largest **ROASTING PANS** and **BAKING TRAYS** that will fit into your oven. If possible, they should be sturdy enough to sit on the stove, for making gravies and sauces after roasting.

EXTRA-WIDE FOIL or turkey foil. The thick sort, not the cheap, thin sort that tears if you so much as look at it. For lidding and roasting.

Nonstick **PARCHMENT PAPER** and **PLASTIC WRAP**, for baking without greasing pans and for covering food made in advance, respectively. If you don't want to buy plastic wrap, use upturned plates and baking sheets to cover bowls and dishes. It is useful when wrapping pie dough and covering bowls of rising bread dough, though.

A big **COLANDER**. For draining rice or pasta, potatoes or noodles, or for rinsing.

A really large stockpot-type **PAN** with a lid. For making soups and stocks on the stovetop. A big Le Creuset-style casserole is also invaluable.

A very long **WOODEN SPOON** and ladle. For the stockpot pan.

A good supply of heavy-duty and large **CUTTING BOARDS**. A few, if possible, so you can chop different food groups hygienically and save washing up until you have finished prepping.

Large springform **CAKE PANS**, tart pans with removable bottoms, and pie dishes. Obviously, this depends greatly on what you will be baking, but I consider anything above 9 inches in diameter to be large. You can rent cake pans from cake decorating stores if you would rather not buy them. You might want to bake a cake in a different-shaped pan; in which case the following is good to know: square pans hold about one-quarter more again of the quantity as round pans of the same size. So, cooking times will increase for square pans, but the oven temperature should remain the same. These pans will hold the same amount of batter:

> 8 inches round = 7 inches square
> 9 inches round = 8 inches square
> 11 inches round = 10½ inches square

A big, heavy-bottomed, nonstick or cast-iron **SKILLET**. Spend as much as you can afford on a great skillet. You will use it all the time.

Food-safe, **PLASTIC CONTAINERS** with lids for storing, transporting, and marinating. They aren't pretty. Hide them in a cupboard.

At least a couple of really big **PLASTIC MIXING BOWLS**. You can pick these up very cheaply. Again, they are not attractive and you won't want to show them off, but they are incredibly useful for tossing salads, marinating, brining, mixing batters, and making dough.

SPARE TABLES. Trestle tables or foldaway tables are just fine. Cover them with tablecloths if they are less than beautiful.

For blending soups, vegetables, and sauces in their pans, you'll need a **HAND BLENDER**. To be perfectly honest, I am wedded to my lovely (safe) freestanding blender, due in part to a minor accident with a hand blender a few years ago. However, if the price of an upright blender is prohibitive, a hand blender is a fantastic thing. Do unplug it when you finish using it.

A **MANDOLIN**, as extolled in the Cozy Weekend Away chapter, will prove its worth if you ever make potatoes à la dauphinoise or shredded salads for more than two. A good-value, plastic model will be more than adequate.

If you have a birthday, wedding, or anniversary present due and you are a fan of all things sweet and frozen, an **ICE-CREAM MAKER** is the thing to hint at. I have a deep love for mine, and it makes short work of whipping up delectable, smooth ices with none of that incessant "beating every two hours until set" business. Pour in your chilled base mix, switch it on, and you should have a frozen treat in twenty minutes or so. The results make a mockery of overpriced tubs. The only negatives are the whirring noise (I frequently sit mine in another room and close the door while it churns) and the sheer weight of the thing, but we must bear such crosses in return for good ice cream.

A NOTE ON THESE RECIPES

* Spoon measurements are level, unless stated.
* If not specified, butter should be salted.
* Eggs are large, unless stated. Please do buy free-range.
* The recipes have been tested using whole milk and whole dairy, unless stated.
* "Salt" refers to flakes of sea salt; "pepper" refers to freshly ground black peppercorns.
* Ovens run at varying temperatures. The recipes were tested using a thermometer for accuracy.

VIETNAMESE BRIDAL SHOWER FOR 8

BEEF IN BETEL LEAVES | VIETNAMESE TABLE SALAD AND PICKLED VEGETABLES | STICKY QUAIL IN HONEY & FIVE SPICE | *Green mango salad* | BAKED WHITE CHOCOLATE & RHUBARB CUSTARDS | PINEAPPLE AND GINGER FIZZ

The bridal theme is merely a suggestion; this dainty menu would be a dream for any spring supper. Haphazard and charming might not be your thing, but it certainly makes for a pretty table. Flatware and chopsticks can be amassed in a pot in the middle, or tied loosely with twine at each place setting. Nothing needs to match.

Spring blooms, herbs, and tealights in jam jars look beautiful; basil and lemon verbena will both smell delicious and ward off evening bugs to boot. If you have the wherewithal to eat outside, fairy lights threaded through greenery or a few paper lanterns on the ground never go amiss.

Spread the preparation over a couple of days to make things easier on yourself. The custards can be made two days ahead, as can the pickles and dipping sauce (which doubles as a salad dressing). The salads come to no harm if put together an hour or two before serving and kept, covered, in a cool place.

Despite all this, I suggest getting some help from a willing minion. Although nothing is particularly complicated, there is rather a lot of chopping and shredding. Such is usually the way with Southeast Asian dishes. Soldier on, however, and you will be duly rewarded with an exceptional supper.

Instead of serving everything savory at once, as intended, you could start with the beef and treat the quail as a main with the green mango salad. For vegetarians, separately marinate cubes of firm tofu in the quail marinade for a few hours. Roast in a moderate oven, turning now and then, until golden and sticky. Knock out an extra dipping sauce using light soy in place of fish sauce. It won't be the same, but it will be no less delicious.

BEEF IN BETEL LEAVES
(BO LA LOT)

MAKES ABOUT 48 (6 EACH)
PREP 30 MINUTES
COOK 10 MINUTES

5 tablespoons peanuts, toasted
   and crushed or chopped
1½ pounds coarsely minced beef
2 garlic cloves, minced
2 lemon grass stalks, bulbous
   ends only, minced
3 scallions, white parts only,
   minced (use the
   green parts for the quail,
   see page 21)
1 teaspoon curry powder
1 tablespoon fish sauce
2 teaspoons superfine sugar
½ teaspoon freshly ground white
   pepper
45-55 large betel leaves (you'll
   need 2 large bunches)

DARK GREEN, HEART-SHAPED BETEL LEAVES CAN BE FOUND IN THAI OR VIETNAMESE FOOD STORES. They will be nestling in refrigerator cases, wrapped in cellophane packages alongside the herbs. Use any duds in stir-fries and just concentrate on stuffing the large, unblemished leaves for your own sanity. While you're in the store, look for Vietnamese (sometimes labeled "Madras") curry powder. It's sweet, bright, highly fragrant, and perfect with the beef.

Combine 3 tablespoons of the crushed peanuts with all the remaining ingredients except the betel leaves. Season with a pinch of salt. Take a betel leaf and lay it shiny side down on a counter. Take 1 heaped dessert spoon of the beef mixture, rolling it into a fat log. Place this on the pointed end of the betel leaf and roll up tightly, piercing the stalk end through the leaf to secure. This is nowhere near as tricky as it sounds, but the truly inept could use toothpicks. Repeat to make 48 rolls; you will get quicker and more dextrous as you go.

Place a large griddle or skillet over high heat. Griddle or fry the betel rolls in the pan—they won't stick—until slightly charred on all sides, in batches if necessary, keeping the cooked rolls warm in a low oven. The leaves will soften, wrinkle, and turn shinier still. Serve about 6 per person, scattered with the remaining peanuts and sitting on a bed of rice noodles and Table Salad (see page 18).

VIETNAMESE DIPPING SAUCE
(NUOC CHAM)

MAKES ENOUGH FOR 8
PREP 5 MINUTES

4 tablespoons superfine sugar
6 tablespoons rice wine vinegar
6 tablespoons Vietnamese fish
   sauce *(nuoc mam)*
juice of 2 limes
2-3 Thai chilies, minced, or
   to taste

THE UBIQUITOUS (IN VIETNAM, ANYWAY) *NUOC CHAM* IS BASED ON GOOD-QUALITY *NUOC MAM*, VIETNAMESE FISH SAUCE. Versions abound, but this one makes an excellent entry-level sauce to be adjusted to taste. Variations include adding minced garlic and/or ginger and/or finely shredded pickled carrot and radish. It also doubles as a dressing for Asian salads.

Gently heat the sugar with the vinegar, fish sauce, and ⅔ cup water, until the sugar dissolves. Do not let the mixture boil. Let cool. Add the lime juice and chilies, depending on your preference for spiciness. Serve in little pots or dishes, or use as a salad dressing.

VIETNAMESE TABLE SALAD

MAKES ENOUGH FOR 8 AS AN ACCOMPANIMENT
PREP 10 MINUTES

9 ounces fine rice noodles
small bunch of cilantro
small bunch of mint
small bunch of Vietnamese mint
    or Thai basil (if available)
large handful of perilla
    (if available)
2 heads round lettuce, leaves
    separated, rinsed and dried
1 cucumber, sliced on the
    diagonal
1 carambola, sliced (optional)
Pickled Vegetables (see below)
Vietnamese Dipping Sauce
    (see page 16)

A VIETNAMESE-STYLE TABLE SALAD IS THERE TO WRAP, roll, and generally customize your supper. Use the larger lettuce leaves as vessels, filling them with any combination of rice noodles, fragrant herbs, a tangle of Pickled Vegetables (see below), and perhaps a slice of carambola or cucumber. Add your main event —*Bo La Lot* or a boneless piece of quail (see pages 16 and 21)—roll the leaf around the filling, then dip in Nuoc Cham and eat.

Soak the noodles in hot water for a few minutes, according to the package directions, then refresh under cold water and drain well.

Now either divide everything between individual serving bowls, keeping the components in groups rather than mixing them up, or serve on communal platters for your guests to help themselves.

PICKLED VEGETABLES

MAKES ENOUGH FOR 8 AS AN ACCOMPANIMENT
PREP 10 MINUTES

½ cup superfine sugar
¾ cup rice vinegar
11 ounces carrots, peeled and cut
    into fine sticks
7 ounces daikon (white radish),
    peeled and cut into fine sticks

THESE QUICK PICKLES WILL KEEP, chilled, in their pickling brine for a good couple of weeks.

Combine the sugar and vinegar with scant ½ cup water and a pinch of salt in a bowl, stirring until the sugar dissolves. Add the vegetable sticks and set aside for at least 2 hours to pickle them. Cover and refrigerate if you're going to keep them for longer.

Using your naturally favored hand, hold one chopstick (near the top for added elegance), tucking it in between thumb and first finger so that the tip points diagonally downward. Steady the stick further down toward the tip with the inside of your bent third finger.

Now add the second chopstick, holding it in the same place on the stick, grasping it as you would a pencil, so that both chopstick tips are at the same level. It should be held firmly between the tips of your thumb, index, and middle fingers.

To pick up food, the index and middle fingers should pivot, bringing the second chopstick down to meet the first. Apply pressure with your thumb to hold the chopstick securely.

Practice moving the second chopstick freely, while the first chopstick remains stationary. Your movements will become more precise as you grow familiar with the sensation.

It is considered most impolite to "spear" your food with a chopstick, so if all your attempts to be dextrous end in failure, better to give in and ask for a fork.

STICKY QUAIL IN HONEY AND FIVE SPICE (CHIME)

NOBODY IN THEIR RIGHT MIND WOULD OPT TO DEEP-FRY FOR EIGHT IN THE MIDDLE OF DINNER, especially in a nice dress. So, on this occasion, I have recommended grilling the quail. They will take on beautiful charred tones, and the skin will caramelize and become crisp.

If you are cooking this for supper rather than a party, however, do try deep-frying the quails. Submerge three at a time in peanut oil, patting them dry first. Check that the oil is hot with a scrap of bread; it should turn golden in about 30 seconds. Fry the little birds for about 5 minutes, until golden, drain well, and serve hot. Incidentally, a platter of honeyed quails makes a lovely substitute for the humble burger in case you were looking for grill inspiration.

Using a pair of sharp scissors, snip through the backbone of each quail, opening out flat. Rinse under the faucet and dry thoroughly with paper towels.

Grate the ginger finely, skin and all. Gather up the gratings and, holding your hands over a bowl, squeeze to release all the liquid. Discard the dry gratings. Add all the other marinade ingredients to the bowl, stir well, and slather over the quails. Cover the bowl and set aside to chill for a few hours or overnight. A minimum of 2 hours will do, if that's all you have.

When ready to cook, heat the oven to 400°F and line a large roasting pan with foil. Place a large griddle pan over fierce heat until it's positively smoking. Working in two or three batches, shake the quails free of any excess marinade and griddle, skin side-down first, for a minute or so on each side, until burnished brown and charred in places. Transfer to the roasting pan, skin side up, as you go. When all have been griddled, pour any leftover marinade over the birds and roast for 10 minutes, until just cooked through but still juicy. Meanwhile, mix together all the ingredients for the dipping sauce and place in a small bowl.

Pile the quails up on a platter, scatter with shredded scallions, and serve with the dipping sauce on the side.

SERVES 8
PREP 20 MINUTES, PLUS MARINATING
COOK ABOUT 12 MINUTES

8 quails
3 scallions, green parts only, shredded

FOR THE MARINADE
thumb-size piece of fresh gingerroot
2½ tablespoons dark soy sauce
2½ tablespoons runny honey
2 garlic cloves, crushed
½ teaspoon five spice powder
2 tablespoons Shaoxing rice wine

FOR THE LEMON AND PEPPER DIPPING SAUCE
juice of 2 lemons
2 teaspoons freshly ground white pepper
1 teaspoon sea salt

GREEN MANGO SALAD
(GOI XOAI XANH)

I COULD LIVE ON THIS. Customize as you wish with shrimp, strips of pork belly, shredded chicken, roasted rice, fried shallots, crushed peanuts in place of the slightly inauthentic cashews, even dried shrimps or squid (found in Vietnamese grocery stores). As part of this menu, I've kept the components pure and simple.

If you find yourself in the aforementioned Vietnamese grocer, or any good Thai food store, you can pick up a shredding tool very cheaply. They look like corrugated swivel peelers. If you don't have one, use the shredder attachment on a food processor, or peel the carrots and mango into thin strips with a vegetable peeler, then stack them into piles and slice into long thin sticks.

Make sure your Nuoc Cham has a good chili kick, adding a finely sliced Thai chili or two to remedy things should it fall short. Sweet, salt, sour, and hot flavors should all be pronounced and balanced.

If your mangoes are very firm and dry, shred them into fine sticks. If they have any give at all when pressed, they will be too juicy for shredding, so slice or pare (using a swivel-blade vegetable peeler) into wide but delicate strips.

Combine all the ingredients except the cashews and set aside for 20 minutes or so before serving, so the flavors can get to know each other. Scatter with the nuts just before serving to add crunch.

SERVES 8
PREP 20 MINUTES

4 large green mangoes, peeled
2 carrots, scrubbed and finely
    shredded
handful of Vietnamese mint, Thai
    basil, mint, or cilantro, or a
    combination, shredded
6 tablespoons Nuoc Cham
    dipping sauce (see page 16)
3 tablespoons cashews, roasted
    and crushed

BAKED WHITE CHOCOLATE AND RHUBARB CUSTARDS

IF YOU HAVE THE TIME, MAKE THESE LIGHT AND WOBBLY CUSTARDS A DAY OR TWO AHEAD; it will spread the load. I've scented them with vanilla, but half a dozen cracked green cardamom pods will also marry beautifully with both the white chocolate and the rhubarb. The rhubarb leaves behind a stunning pink syrup; perfect as a base for drinks: top off with champagne, elderflower pressé, or seltzer.

Preheat the oven to 400°F. Place the rhubarb in a roasting dish, scatter with the sugar, cover with foil, and roast for 25 minutes, until tender but still holding its shape. Using a slotted spoon so most of the syrup is left behind, divide the rhubarb between 8 ovenproof dishes, pots, or ramekins, and chill.

Heat the cream, milk, salt, and vanilla bean in a pan until steaming but not boiling. Remove from the heat and set aside to infuse for 20 minutes. Reduce the oven temperature to 350°F. Chop 7 ounces of the white chocolate quite finely and set the remainder aside. Return the cream mixture to the heat and bring up to just below boiling point, as before.

Whisk the egg yolks and sugar in a heatproof mixing bowl until pale and thickened. Remove the steaming pan from the heat and add the chopped chocolate, stirring to dissolve. Gradually pour this onto the egg yolks, whisking. Pass the mixture through a fine strainer into a pitcher to remove any strands of egg and the vanilla bean. (Rinse and dry the bean, then use it to flavor jars of sugar.)

Set the rhubarb pots in a deep roasting pan. Very carefully pour the custard onto the rhubarb, slowly-slowly so as not to disturb the pink layer, filling to near the top, then cover each pot with a square of foil. Boil a kettle. Place the roasting pan in the middle of the oven, then pull the oven rack out and fill the pan with boiling water to reach halfway up each custard pot.

Bake for 35 to 40 minutes, until the custard is just set but still jiggles in the center. Let cool, then chill for at least 3 hours or overnight.

Scrape a sharp knife, held at an angle, over the flat base of the reserved chocolate to make large shavings and scrolls. Pile these shavings messily onto each custard pot and serve.

SERVES 8
PREP 30 MINUTES
COOK 1 HOUR 15 MINUTES, PLUS 20 MINUTES INFUSING AND AT LEAST 3 HOURS CHILLING

FOR THE RHUBARB
1 pound 10 ounces pink rhubarb, trimmed and chopped into 1¼-inch lengths
⅔ cup superfine sugar

FOR THE CUSTARDS
2 cups light cream
generous 1 cup whole milk
pinch of salt
1 vanilla bean, split
11 ounces white chocolate
6 egg yolks
3 tablespoons superfine sugar

GENERAL RULES
when cooking for a crowd

Or, in other words, what I have learned from attempting to cater from a home kitchen.

PLAN TO COOK VERY LITTLE FRIED FOOD

A few odds and ends are fine—a hot and crisp garnish for a salad perhaps—but anything more tends to mean a flustered, oil-spattered cook and kitchen, greasy food (because of the sheer quantities involved), and a general last-minute panic. Instead, use a low oven to braise and slowly roast. Toast nuts, seeds, and bread in advance, to add crunch and a variety of textures.

TRY TO FREE UP THE OVEN FOR THE LAST TWENTY MINUTES

or so before you plan to eat, ready to be used for plate-warming, reheating, and so on. Roasts should be tented with foil and left to rest; braises and stews will be volcanically hot, so a few minutes sitting on the counter with a lid on will not harm them. Try not to cook too many items—or any at all—that need to go from oven to plate with lightning speed.

USE YOUR FREEZER . . .

So much can be made and kept frozen until needed, even if it is just stocks and ice creams. Free up space in the refrigerator and the freezer, ready for the extra load. If necessary, beg, borrow, or hire extra room from a friend or neighbor. Temporary refrigerators and the like can be set up in a garage, barn, stable, or shed with electricity Incidentally, I keep large quantities of nuts and spices in the freezer to preserve their delicate oils.

DON'T OVERCOMPLICATE

Yes, be relatively ambitious and make that smoked pastrami or delightful chicken pie, but keep any extras simple. Let good food speak for itself.

PREPARE IN ADVANCE AND MAKE IN ADVANCE

When cooking for a crowd, never, ever leave everything until the last minute. Spread the prep out over a few days so that it doesn't feel so arduous, and make anything that won't suffer, or might even improve, ahead of time. Chopped onion and other vegetables can be stored in the refrigerator in airtight containers; dressings can be made; pastries chilled; tart crusts blind-baked . . .

Simplify if needed

If you look at a menu of recipes and know you won't be able to cope with everything, don't. Buy dessert or ask a friend to make it. Replace one of the sides with a green salad. Buy good bread.

AND YOUR CUPBOARD

Shopping is an awful lot easier if you can knowingly build up a good stock of the items you'll need regularly, like olive oil, spices, vinegars, mustards, and pickles. If you happen to be passing, say, a Thai store, and you know you'll need kaffir lime leaves at some point, buy them at the time and freeze them. Be an opportunist.

DELEGATE, BORROW, AND GET HELP WITH ANYTHING YOU CAN

Taking care of all drinks on top of the food is a lot of work, so ask a knowledgeable friend to take the task on, in return for a good supper. Don't skimp on the quantities; you can return excess bottles of wine and beer. (But if you think you might, don't place them in ice buckets until you know you'll need them, or their labels will peel off.)

Set up early

Set up tables, if needed, and assemble chairs, flatware, glasses, and any decorations you want well in advance. Think of this as dressing a set for a play. Trying to lay the table attractively with two minutes to spare before a crowd arrives isn't exactly calming, so these are the ideal jobs to delegate to a willing friend a day or two beforehand.

DON'T BE AFRAID TO LET LARGE JOINTS OF MEAT REST,

tented with foil. They will not turn stone cold in thirty minutes.

EMBRACE YOUR INNER CONTROL FREAK:

budget, make lists, make more lists, be sure you have all the equipment needed and write a rough timetable for your prep and cooking. Wear a hands-free headset and a power suit if it helps.

ASK FAMILY AND FRIENDS FOR HELP WITH ADVANCE PREPARATION AND SETTING UP

Don't be fastidious; if you don't have enough, borrow chairs, cooking equipment, trestle tables, flatware, glasses, or crockery. A good, relaxed, party atmosphere is far more important than matching flatware.

MAKE DESSERT IN ADVANCE

At least there will be something edible and ready to go; if all else fails, offer lots of wine and a lovely dessert. Rename it a sweet party.

MAKE USE OF THE INTERNET AND HOME DELIVERY

Ordering food online and by mail order has changed my life, and a large order with some companies can mean you get a free delivery. Take full advantage.

ARTFULLY CONVINCE GUESTS TO SERVE THEMSELVES

With a bit of style and charm, you can set up food (beautifully), on separate tables or on platters, ready for everyone to make up their own platefuls. Cunningly disguise this as a "fun!" "interactive!" activity and you won't have to assemble twenty perfect platefuls from a tiny kitchen. (See pages 18–21, 82, and 159 for some elegant examples of how to manage this.)

FINALLY, TRY TO STAY CALM

If everything goes wrong, it really isn't the end of the world. Make an emergency trip for bread and sausages or cheese and ham, and have a glass of wine.

PINEAPPLE AND GINGER FIZZ

CHOOSE SWEET-SMELLING, YELLOW PINEAPPLES FOR THIS; it is important to be sure that they aren't sour or acidic. If the fruit is ripe, a spiky leaf should come away easily when tugged.

Infuriating to clean as they may be, if you have a juicer lurking at the back of a cupboard, it will make short work of two sweet pineapples and a touch of ginger. A blender and a strainer will do the job too, so I've given directions for each.

If you don't like ginger, leave it out, or replace it with a handful of mint leaves to make tropical mojitos.

Trim and pare the tough skin from each pineapple. Only bother to core them if you are using a blender; a juicer will make short work of the woody centers. Cut the flesh into chunks. If you own a juicer, feed the pineapple in with the ginger. Pour into a large pitcher with ⅔ cup iced water, mixing thoroughly.

If using a blender, chop the unpeeled ginger roughly. Working in three batches, pulse the pineapple and ginger together with scant ¼ cup water for each batch. Pour through a strainer into a large pitcher, discarding the pulp.

Either way, chill the juice until serving, for up to 8 hours.

To make each cocktail, vigorously shake the pineapple and ginger juice, rum, and sugar together with a few ice cubes. If you don't own a cocktail shaker—I certainly don't—a Thermos flask or large, lidded glass jar works perfectly. Strain into a tall glass filled with crushed ice, topping off with soda water to taste. Decorate with edible flowers, a lime slice, or a fresh pineapple slice.

MAKES COCKTAILS UNTIL THE RUM RUNS OUT
PREP 15 MINUTES

FOR THE FRESH PINEAPPLE AND GINGER JUICE
2 large, fragrant and sweet pineapples
chubby thumb-size piece of fresh gingerroot

FOR EACH GLASS
scant ¼ cup fresh pineapple and ginger juice
2-3 tablespoons light rum, or more, to taste
½-1 teaspoon light brown sugar, to taste
crushed ice
soda water
edible flowers, lime, or pineapple slices, to garnish

VEGETARIAN GARDEN BRUNCH FOR 8

EGGS EN COCOTTE WITH GOAT CHEESE, TARRAGON, AND TOMATO | **HERB FOUGASSE AND FIG AND MOZZARELLA PIZZAS** *Toasted muesli bowls* | SPRING JUICE BAR | LEMON AND ROSEMARY TART

If luck keeps the showers at bay, and you have the wherewithal, this feast of a menu is perfect to serve around a big, outdoor table. The difference in food bills between cooking a menu based on meat or fish, compared to a vegetarian spread, never ceases to amaze me. Reason enough, quite apart from the nourishing and celebratory recipes, to make this brunch. Whether you're cooking for a party of vegetarians or not, I wouldn't even mention the absence of meat; nobody will think to miss or notice anything. If the very idea of going meatless horrifies you—though I can't think why it should—drape prosciutto over the cooked pizzas or top each baked egg cup with a shard of crisp bacon.

Getting in a panic before a supposedly relaxed brunch isn't particularly enjoyable, and there is a lot to do, so make the tart and the bread dough at your leisure, at least a day in advance—ideal if you plan to eat on a Sunday. Likewise, get the muesli under way the night before and assemble your fruits and vegetables for juicing. You can even prepare the eggs the night before, up to the point of covering each cup with foil. On the day, cook the fougasse first, then let the eggs come up to room temperature for twenty minutes while you turn the oven down ready for them. Get somebody to help with the juices while you fire the oven back up, ready to finish off the pizzas to order.

A hearty brunch such as this will set you up for the whole day—I doubt anyone will want so much as a snack afterward—so let everyone know they should arrive hungry. Stagger the food so as not to overwhelm, and to make things easier for you. I start serving the eggs around late morning or even midday on a lazy weekend day, and don't set any particular finishing time.

The odd glass of champagne shouldn't be ruled out.

EGGS EN COCOTTE
WITH GOAT CHEESE, TARRAGON, AND TOMATO

THESE HANDSOME EGGS MANAGE TO BE BOTH ESPECIALLY SPRINGLIKE AND EXACTLY WHAT YOU'D WANT FOR BRUNCH. There is no need to be too thorough when seeding the tomatoes, just get the bulk out. The seeds and surrounding jelly hold so much flavor that I rarely remove them, but unfortunately, they would dilute the cream too much in this case. Besides, the charming—and whole—cherry tomatoes release extra pops of sweetness to set the goat cheese off beautifully.

Preheat the oven to 350°F. Lightly butter the insides of 8 ovenproof cups or ramekins.

Cut a shallow cross in the base of all the medium tomatoes and place them in a bowl. Boil a kettle and pour the boiled water over the tomatoes to cover. Leave them for barely a minute—their skins should begin to lift and curl—then drain the water away and peel off the skins. Cut the tomatoes in half and scoop out the seeds with a teaspoon. Cut each half into two petals.

Divide the tomato petals, cherry tomatoes, cream, most of the tarragon, and most of the goat cheese between the cups or ramekins. Season well with salt and pepper. Crack an egg into each and finish with the remaining tarragon and goat cheese. Sit the cups in a roasting pan and bake for 15 to 20 minutes, depending on whether you prefer a runny or a set yolk. Serve with teaspoons and Herb Fougasse loaves (see page 34), for dipping.

SERVES 8
PREP 15 MINUTES
COOK 15 MINUTES

a little soft unsalted butter
6 ripe, medium tomatoes
large handful of mixed cherry
     tomatoes
1¼ cups light cream
leaves from 3 sprigs of tarragon,
     chopped
5 ounces soft goat cheese log,
     sliced
8 very fresh, large eggs

HERB FOUGASSE AND FIG AND MOZZARELLA PIZZAS

ONE DOUGH, TWO IMPRESSIVE OUTCOMES . . . AND A KITCHEN THAT SMELLS HEAVENLY. This is one to make if you're selling your house and want to increase its appeal. Obviously, if you would like to make just the bread or just the pizzas, divide the dough quantities in half. Warming the flour and mixing bowl in a very low oven prior to mixing the sponge will really get the yeast going and adds a pleasingly sour flavor. Assuming you will be making this for a late morning brunch and will be unwilling to get up at daybreak to start the dough, I suggest you make it the day before and allow it to rise slowly overnight.

I highly recommend a pizza stone to cook the pizzas; it will make a marked difference in the texture of the crust in a conventional oven, and they are relatively inexpensive. Preheat the stone for as long as you can on a shelf near the top of the oven (I'd pop it in to preheat before cooking the eggs, just to give it a head start). Ease a flat baking sheet under the paper each proofed pizza sits on, pull the oven shelf out, and carefully slide each pizza from the baking sheet onto the hot stone, paper and all.

Combine half the flour with the yeast and about 1 cup hand-hot water in a large mixing bowl. Beat with a wooden spoon, or with the paddle attachment of a mixer, for 3 minutes or so. Cover the bowl with oiled plastic wrap and set aside in a warm, not hot, place for 3 to 4 hours. I favor a barely-switched-on oven. Be careful, anything more than warm will kill the yeast and stop it rising. The sponge (for this is what you have made) will rise up and collapse back under its own weight during this time.

Add the remaining flour and scant ¼ cup more hand-hot water along with the salt and oil to make a very soft dough. Knead by hand on a lightly floured counter, or in a mixer using a dough hook, for 10 minutes, until elastic and smooth. The mixture has a relatively loose consistency and is all the better for it, so don't be tempted to add too much extra flour. Keep persevering, and the dough will become less sticky as you knead and develop the gluten in the flour.

Either cover the bowl with oiled plastic wrap as before, or place the dough in a large food-grade bag, into which you have drizzled a little oil to prevent it from sticking. Force out the air and leave space for the dough to rise when sealing tightly. Place the bag or bowl in the refrigerator and let rise slowly overnight. Remove from the

MAKES 2 LARGE PIZZAS AND 4 SMALL FOUGASSE LOAVES
PREP 40 MINUTES, PLUS 4½ TO 6½ HOURS AND OVERNIGHT RISING
COOK ABOUT 15 MINUTES FOR THE FOUGASSE; 10 TO 12 MINUTES PER PIZZA

FOR THE DOUGH
4¼ cups white bread flour, plus more to dust
1½ ounces fresh yeast or ¾ ounce dried yeast (normal or fast acting)
2 teaspoons sea salt, plus more to scatter over before baking
5 tablespoons extra-virgin olive oil, plus more to drizzle
coarse semolina, to dust

CONTINUED . . .

FOR THE FOUGASSE
good handful of basil leaves
   or mixed soft herb leaves,
   chopped

FOR THE PIZZAS
6 plump figs, trimmed and sliced
3 balls of mozzarella, buffalo or
   cow, drained and roughly torn
good handful of basil leaves

refrigerator at least 30 minutes before opening, to take the chill off. If you intend to cook the dough on the same day, a quicker rise will be called for: cover or bag it and return to the warm place to rise for an hour, or until doubled in size.

Punch the dough firmly to deflate it and divide it in half. Cover the half destined to make pizza bases—to stop it forming a crust—and set aside at room temperature while you make the fougasse.

To make the fougasse loaves, prepare a couple of large, flat baking sheets by oiling them (sparingly) and sprinkling lightly with semolina. Knead the basil, or herbs of your choice, into the dough and divide it into four pieces. Roll each out on a lightly floured counter to form a 1¼–1½-inch thick oval shape. Transfer two ovals to each baking sheet and, working one loaf at a time, cut a short vertical line up the center. Now cut three short, diagonal slashes up each half, as if you were scoring the ribs in a simple leaf from near the central lines. Gently pull each cut apart with your hands, to form oblong holes in the dough. Cover the loaves with damp, clean dish towels or oiled plastic wrap, and set aside in a warm place to puff up for an hour. Meanwhile, preheat the oven to 450°F. Drizzle each fougasse with a little olive oil, scatter with sea salt, and bake for 15 minutes or so, until pale golden and risen. Cool on wire racks until just warm or at room temperature. Slice each loaf into soldiers at the table, ready to dip into the baked eggs.

To make the pizzas, have a couple of large, flat baking sheets (flat so that you can easily slide off the cooked pizzas) and two large squares of nonstick parchment paper ready.

Divide the pizza dough into two. Using a rolling pin and a little extra flour, roll and stretch each half out to form a rough circle. The dough should be very thin, about ¼ inch if you can.

Place a square of parchment paper onto each baking sheet and scatter lightly with semolina. Carefully transfer a pizza base onto each. Being careful to leave a border, cover the base with half the figs and mozzarella, finishing with a few basil leaves, a scattering of salt, and a drizzle of olive oil. Let rise at room temperature for 20 to 30 minutes. Preheat the oven to 450°F and position an oven rack near the top. Cook the pizzas one at a time, for about 10 to 12 minutes each, until the base is turning golden and the top is bubbling. If you have a pizza stone, preheat it as early as possible and slide each risen pizza onto it, as described in the recipe introduction. Cut the cooked pizza into wedges—I find kitchen scissors most effective—scatter with a few more basil leaves and serve hot, before quickly getting the next one into the oven.

TOASTED MUESLI BOWLS

TROPICAL FRUIT IS STILL FABULOUS AT THIS TIME OF YEAR, particularly the mangoes, of which the honeyed Indian Alphonso is most certainly king.

I favor finding a delicious, hearty organic store-bought mix if you find one you love. You can use any hearty muesli mix too. If you, or anyone you want to make this for, is gluten intolerant, I have also had very good results using purely quinoa flakes (from health food stores).

The toasting step ramps up the nuttiness of the oats nicely and lends them a firmer texture that will weather an overnight soaking. Do toast the nuts and seeds; it makes a world of difference.

As with any muesli variation, you'll need to start this recipe the night before, but then most of the work will be done.

Toast the slivered almonds and seeds in a large skillet, shaking it often until they begin to turn golden. Add the coconut for the last minute or so, it will toast fast so remove the pan from the heat before golden turns to burned. Tip into a bowl and set aside. Return the pan to the heat and add a third or half of the oats or muesli, using a wooden spoon to keep everything moving. Keep cooking for about 5 minutes, until the oats turn a light brown and smell toasted. Tip into a large bowl and repeat once or twice more with the remaining oats.

Peel the mangoes with a swivel peeler and slice the fat cheeks from each, cutting either side of the flat stone. Take care as a peeled mango is rather slippery. Cut the remaining flesh from around the seed and dice it up. Combine with the grated apple, toasted oats or muesli mix, apple juice, and half the toasted nut and seed mix, stirring well. Cover and chill overnight, or for a bare minimum of 1 hour if that's really all you have.

In the morning, divide the mixture between serving bowls and offer chopped tropical fruit, milk, yogurt, and the remaining toasted nut and seed mixture to spoon or pour over. Each bowl can then be customized to taste. You may wish to finish with a drizzle of honey, but the fruit is likely to be sweet enough.

MAKES 8 GENEROUS BOWLFULS
PREP 20 MINUTES, PLUS OVERNIGHT SOAKING
COOK ABOUT 12 TO 17 MINUTES, DEPENDING ON HOW MANY BATCHES YOU TOAST THE OATS INTO

½ cup slivered almonds
generous ⅓ cup pumpkin or sunflower seeds
2 tablespoons unsweetened coconut flakes, or unsweetened dry shredded coconut
scant 4¾ cups rolled oats or muesli
3 large or 4 small mangoes
4 crunchy eating apples, cored and coarsely grated
scant 3 cups fresh apple and mango juice, or apple juice
peeled and chopped tropical fruits, such as banana, lychee, pineapple, kiwi, and more mango, to serve
about 2 cups cold milk, to serve
generous 1 cup organic yogurt, to serve
mild honey, to serve (optional)

SPRING JUICE BAR

EACH MAKES 1 PITCHER
PREP 10 TO 15 MINUTES PER
  JUICE

PURPLE
4 large beets, quartered
5 large carrots
4 pears, quartered
fat thumb-size piece of fresh
  gingerroot
squeeze of lemon juice, to finish

ROSE
10 large oranges, peeled
3½ cups early strawberries,
  hulled

GREEN
6 apples, quartered
3 celery stalks
14 ounces white grapes, removed
  from their stalks
2 handfuls of spinach leaves
handful of mint leaves
squeeze of lime, to finish

TO MAKE THE FRESH JUICES AS WRITTEN, YOU'LL NEED A JUICER. If you have one sulking at the back of the cupboard (I know—they are hellish to clean), this is the time to dust it off. I buy cheap fruit and vegetables at my local market or grocery store, going with whatever looks best, as it's usually better value than in most supermarkets.

Coerce a willing guest, family member, or other half into making the juices for you when needed; they involve nothing more than feeding the prepared fruit and vegetables into the juicer, pressing down firmly with the plunger bit. Don't forget to put a large container by the collecting spout for the juice!

If you don't own a juicer and can't borrow one, just buy several different, ready-made, fresh juices and chill them down thoroughly. Combine on the day-of to make your own mixtures. Or squeeze a couple of pitchers of orange juice from fresh oranges.

The following are merely suggestions. Each will fill one pitcher, or about four glasses. Do try other combinations, depending on what's abundant and in season.

Juice each combination in your machine. Stir each juice well before finishing with the citrus (in the case of the purple and green varieties), then pouring them into large pitchers with a little ice. Serve immediately, when the vitamins and minerals are at their most plentiful and beneficial.

Group the juices at one end of the table, encouraging your guests to help themselves before they sit down to eat. Provide spoons or muddlers to stir each glass again before drinking; freshly made juices will naturally separate slightly on sitting.

Wild Foraging

Blooming springtime has much to offer for the amateur to go a-foraging. No trespassing, mind you. My handsome Opinel folding knife serves very well as a collecting tool. I've detailed a small selection of well-known and easily recognized plants below. One final note: if you're not absolutely sure what you're picking, leave it alone and cook some pasta instead.

A FEW GEMS TO GET ACQUAINTED WITH:

ELDERFLOWERS

Flat and frothy heads of tiny white blossom adorn bushy (usually), low-growing elderflower trees in late spring and early summer. They are plentiful in cities and the country in most areas. Look for them in hedges and along the edge of woodland; you will be able to detect the blooms' musky perfume from some distance.

Use the flower heads immediately, shaken free of any tiny insects, to make an intense elderflower cordial for drinks, jellies, and sorbets. Or infuse barely scalded cream with fresh elderflowers, strain, and use to make English possets, pannacottas, mousses, custards, and ice creams.

Coated in a light batter and fried, the heads make a delightful, airy fritter. I adore these, dusted with confectioners' sugar, as a hot accompaniment to homemade elderflower ice cream.

RAMPS AND WILD GARLIC

In rural Sussex, where I'm from, there is much shaking of heads at London folk paying for ramps and wild garlic leaves by the box or bag. Why would you when they grow so freely below hedges, in damp woodlands, and along river banks? Follow your nose; wild garlic gently reeks of . . . garlic. Unsurprisingly. Look for elegant and pointed, gray-green and shiny leaves, rather like tulip leaves in appearance. The white flower heads bob about on vertical stems and resemble large chive flowers. Cut from near the base, leaving

each plant with enough leaves to keep growing, and store in the refrigerator for a few days, loosely wrapped in damp newspaper. Use both leaves and flowers in stir-fries and sauces and, when very young, in salads. Ramp pesto—made by pounding the leaves, pine nuts, Parmesan, and olive oil together—is a joy with pasta and in paninis. Or stuff chicken breasts with soft cheese and the chopped leaves then wrap in larger leaves, followed by a layer of prosciutto. Roast until cooked through.

PRIMROSE FLOWERS AND VIOLETS

Tread carefully when gathering blossoms from primroses and their ilk . . . they are often a legally protected flower in the wild so, unless you grew them yourself or are in a private garden with permission from the owner, you definitely shouldn't be taking them. If you are lucky enough to have some in your garden, however, a few of the sweet flowers make a beautiful addition to spring salads. If it appeals, both primroses and violets can be candied—coat in turn with egg white and superfine sugar, then dry—ready to decorate cakes and desserts.

DANDELION LEAVES

Everybody should be able to recognize the ubiquitous and nutrituous dandelion. It must be a rare person who didn't try to tell the time by blowing at a fluffy, round seed head when they were a kid. Speaking of which, I used to detest the plants' bitterness but, as an adult, a few of the young leaves in a mixed salad now appeals greatly. Gather the dark green leaves, which look rather like arugula leaves, from grassland and hedges, cutting from near the base and being sure to wash well before use. The entire plant is edible and the root can be sliced and stir-fried, or sautéed. You could also add the bright yellow and densely petaled flowers to green salads to pretty them up.

CHICKWEED

Chickweed grows vigorously and low to the ground, in a sprawling fashion. The diminutive, spade-shaped leaves adorn slender stems with five-petaled, white, daisylike flowers at the top. Look out for it in flowerbeds, hedges, and at the edge of woodlands. Snap a stem as a test and, if a milky (rather than clear) sap runs out, it is not chickweed and you shouldn't eat it.

Omelets and frittatas, quiches and tarts, pastas, risottos, soups, stir-fries, sandwiches, and salads will all benefit from chickweed's mildly herby and fresh flavor, not unlike sweet corn when raw, not to mention its high vitamin C content. It will wilt quickly, so only add at the last minute of cooking.

MORELS

Spring mushrooms don't get as much press as their fall cousins but study any sparsely covered ground, as you walk through deciduous woodland, and you might luck out with clusters of morels. The high-domed and dark gray or brown mushroom caps are intricately folded; they're rather like the outside of a human brain! The stalks are low and creamy-white. Morels are easy to spot and difficult to confuse. Once you get used to the woody surroundings, you might even be able to smell their spores in the air, leading you to more mushrooms downwind of the scent.

The best time to hunt is about three days after rainfall and no later than 11 a.m. Take a paper bag to collect your wares and avoid looking just after, or during, frosts—you won't find any then. When you get home, brush away any dirt and leaves rather than washing the morels, then cook as soon as possible. Foaming butter, chopped garlic, and sourdough toast never went amiss where mushrooms are concerned. Another note: a compound in morels reacts with alcohol to cause mild stomach upsets, so don't cook them with much wine and don't drink much with them. Half a glass is the limit, I'm afraid. If in the slightest doubt, leave wild mushrooms well alone. Do err on the side of caution, please.

STINGING NETTLES

Important: Rubber gloves are mandatory when handling nettles.

Identification should be relatively easy with this one. If the leaves and stalks sting, the plant stands at 20 inches to 6½ feet tall, the tiny flowers are green or brownish and the leaves are heart-shaped and raggedy, you have a stinging nettle. Go for the new growth at the top, first snipping off the bitter top pair of leaves, which are pale in color. Like spinach, it takes a lot of nettle to produce any bulk because they cook down so much. The best thing to make is a smooth nettle and potato soup, but a barely wilted and buttery pasta or gnocchi sauce is also a good idea. Risottos work well, or use a few leaves to make a tea said to help with water retention and high blood pressure.

If this subject interests you and you want to take it further, use regional foraging guides with color reference pictures to tell you exactly what grows in the region and in what season. Not only will you widen your horizons, you'll be less likely to confuse nonedibles with edibles.

LEMON AND ROSEMARY TART

SERVES 8 TO 12
PREP 40 MINUTES, PLUS
    CHILLING
COOK 45 MINUTES

FOR THE PIE DOUGH

2½ cups all-purpose flour
½ teaspoon salt
generous ¾ cup confectioners'
    sugar, sifted
¾ cup (1½ sticks) unsalted
    butter, chilled and diced
2 tablespoons minced rosemary
    leaves
3 egg yolks, from chilled eggs

FOR THE FILLING

finely grated zest and juice of
    5 unwaxed lemons
generous 1 cup superfine sugar
4 eggs, plus 6 egg yolks
2 sprigs of rosemary
scant 1 cup unsalted butter,
    cubed

1 tablespoon confectioners' sugar
crème fraîche or whipped cream,
    to serve (optional)

DURING COLLEGE VACATIONS, I MADE THE RIVER CAFÉ'S LEMON TART WITH ALARMING REGULARITY at the Griffin Inn in Sussex. I could probably make the filling in my sleep!

The lemon is pretty perfect on its own, but in my version a judicious amount of rosemary marries beautifully with the citrus. So much so that I always make it this way now. Use a 9-inch diameter round tart pan if you don't have a 8 by 12-inch rectangular one. You'll need to make this the day before to let it firm up. I dispense with caramelizing a dusting of confectioners' sugar across the surface, but don't let that stop you if you're handy with a blowtorch.

Start with the pie dough. Pulse the flour, salt, and sugar in a food processor a couple of times to aerate it. Add the butter and pulse just until the mixture resembles bread crumbs, being careful not to overwork or it will be tough. Sprinkle the rosemary over and add the egg yolks. Pulse again, until the dough starts to clump together. Tip onto a counter and knead lightly, just until smooth. Form into a fat cylinder and wrap in plastic wrap. Chill for at least 1 hour.

Preheat the oven to 350°F. Slice the cylinder into rounds, each no thinner than ⅛ inch. Lay these rounds side-by-side over the bottom and sides of a fluted 8 by 12-inch rectangular tart pan, with a removable bottom. Press the dough out with your fingertips to line the pan evenly, leaving the edges untrimmed and rising slightly above the top of the pan. Prick the bottom with a fork a few times.

Line with a large rectangle of nonstick parchment paper and fill with ceramic baking beans, dried beans, or uncooked rice. Bake for 15 minutes, until the base no longer looks raw, then remove the paper and beans or rice and continue to cook for 5 to 10 minutes more until the pastry is a pale cookie color and looks "sandy" and dry. Remove from the oven and, once cool enough, use a sharp knife to trim the edges flush with the pan, brushing the trimmings away. Gingerly press the removable bottom and work a knife tip into any corners that stick, just until the pastry lifts away. If the pastry welds itself to the pan at this stage, there will be trouble when you come to release it later. Let cool completely in the pan.

To make the filling, whisk the lemon zest and juice, sugar, eggs, egg yolks, and sprigs of rosemary together in a large pan until blended. Don't worry if the rosemary gets caught up in the whisk; it will still be releasing its oils and doing its work.

Set over very low heat and whisk slowly as you add half the butter. Don't stop whisking or let the heat get too high or you'll have scrambled eggs. Once the first lot of butter has been incorporated, add the second, bit by bit. Keep whisking and heating gently until the mixture thickens enough to leave a trail behind the whisk. Remove from the heat and pour through a strainer into a pitcher.

Sit the pitcher in a sink part-filled with cold water. Keep whisking intermittently to prevent a skin forming, until the curd has cooled to body temperature (close your eyes and prod with a clean finger; you shouldn't detect much of a temperature difference). Drape plastic wrap directly over the surface and let cool to room temperature. (A note for nervous cooks: you can make the filling in a heatproof bowl over gently simmering water. It will take longer but is safer.) Pour the filling into the tart shell and smooth the top. Chill for at least 6 hours or overnight to set. Slice into rectangles and dust with confectioners' sugar just before serving. Crème fraîche or whipped cream will cut through the tartness of the lemon.

VACATION WEEKEND AWAY FOR 8

BRUNCH: | **BANANA, DATE, AND MAPLE SMOOTHIE** | *Merguez sausages, spiced potatoes, and eggs* | **LUNCH:** | PORCHETTA STUFFED WITH FARRO | **FARRO AND GREEN BEAN SALAD** | YOUNG BEETS IN PARCELS | APRICOT AND FIRST RASPBERRY LATTICE TART | **FROZEN YOGURT** | *Supper:* | GALETTES DE BLE NOIR KOHLRABI SALAD

A late spring weekend, when the sun feels truly warm for the first time, is one of life's ultimate pleasures. That reassuring moment arrives when the landscape bursts into summer again, leaving short, dark days far behind.

There is an element of risk involved, for the weather might turn on you, sulking in damp clouds, but when the days set fair and fairer still and the nights retain a jab of chill, this can be the very best time to vacation close to home.

You might be cooking in your own home, in which case the following will mercifully not apply. Unless you are housed in luxury and grandeur, cooking in a vacation home can be a challenge, even with a group of friends to share with the creative chores. It is likely that you will not have a particularly well-equipped kitchen; the oven might be archaic. So if you know you will be cooking a tart or a particular cake, take the tin with you; they are usually light to transport. Less portable but still important is a good, large skillet and a couple of sharp kitchen knives (I have never stayed in a rented house with sharp knives). Wrap the blades in several dish towels and tie in place with string. A sharp swivel peeler for vegetables is invaluable, and I will confess to taking my small, light mandolin along to slice salad vegetables. If you don't know if the kitchen has a blender, take a handheld stick blender along; they are very light. Plan to cook one big lunch and one casual supper over the weekend. Take the ingredients and plenty of milk and juices with you. Beyond that, my advice is this: don't get bogged down in shopping, cooking, and cleaning up for the entire weekend. There will be bars serving food, or restaurants. Do a bit of research for a few ideas before you go. Cook a few lovely things but, otherwise, eat leftovers and cheese and crackers; get outside, explore, have fun.

ESSENTIAL KIT
for weekends away

A rental house will have the basics in place. If you're lucky or have splurged, the kitchen might be a palace, replete with every gadget you could ever wish for. Check with the owners first to avoid doubling up, but here are a few useful extras to pack up in a box.

1 A fine Microplane grater It's a rare vacation home that doesn't have a basic grater, but a fine Microplane is light to pack and invaluable. It will tackle cheese, garlic, nutmeg, citrus zests, fresh gingerroot, and chocolate.

2 A liquid measuring cup Often elusive, this is pretty essential for measuring liquids if you plan on doing any baking.

3 Skillet A really good-quality, nonstick skillet—as large as possible—will beat any battered old rental house pan. Use it as a wok and griddle for crêpes, as well as for stir-fries.

4 A balloon whisk For airy batters, egg whites, and smooth sauces.

5 A handheld blender Instead of an upright, for smoothies, soups, and the like; a basic handheld is surprisingly light.

6 A sharp chef's knife Just one, large and sharp, to replace the inevitably blunt selection at the house. Wrap the blade in layers of sturdy dish towels and tie in place to transport safely. (The dish towels will come in useful too.)

7 Plastic food bags, plastic wrap, foil, and nonstick parchment paper Self-explanatory and invaluable.

WHAT YOU DON'T NEED TO TAKE...

1 A **rolling pin**: use a bottle instead.
2 Spoon measurements. Use the flatware available.
3 A **food processor** or mixer. If either or both are at the property, fantastic, but you shouldn't need them. Pie dough can be made and batters whisked by hand for a couple of days with no ill effects.
4 A **mortar and pestle**. Use a jar base.

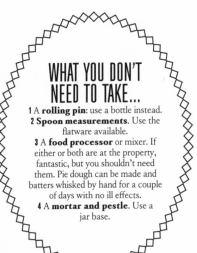

8 A sharp vegetable peeler Of the swivel or Y variety. For peeling vegetables and fruit, or paring and shredding for salads.

9 A small mandolin My cheap Japanese mandolin is invaluable for thinly slicing crunchy vegetables and firm fruits more quickly and uniformly than knives could.

10 Scales A light set of electronic scales for baking; far more accurate than a cheap pair of mechanical scales.

11 Cake pans and pie dishes If you plan on baking anything, take the right pan along. Fudging a cake recipe with the wrong-sized pan in an unfamiliar oven might end in tears.

BRUNCH
BANANA, DATE, AND MAPLE SMOOTHIE

TO CRUSH ICE CUBES, WRAP THEM IN A DISH TOWEL AND BASH energetically with a rolling pin. Thwacking the rolled-up dish towel on a tiled surface or floor also does the job. Both methods also should rid you of any latent tension.

Pulse everything together in a blender. Wrap a dish towel over the lid and hold it firmly as you blend; this should stop any potential overflow getting out of hand. Failing this, use a handheld stick blender and a deep bowl, covering it with a dish towel to prevent splashback.

Taste and add a little more maple syrup if you want, but I doubt you'll think it necessary.

SERVES 4, BUT EASILY DOUBLED
PREP 10 MINUTES

3 large, ripe bananas
handful of Medjool dates, pitted
3 tablespoons rolled oats
2 tablespoons maple syrup, or to taste
scant 2 cups organic yogurt
1¼ cups whole milk
about 12 ice cubes, crushed

AND A VERY FEW USEFUL PANTRY ESSENTIALS.
Take these as well as any ingredients you'll need for specific recipes.
1 A good **olive oil** that will double up for both cooking and salad dressings.
2 A good **balsamic vinegar** for dressings.
3 **White flour** and **baking powder** for impromptu, fluffy breakfast pancakes.
4 **Nuts and seeds** for cereal and oatmeal, to use in baking, or to be toasted and scattered in salads.
5 Sea **salt** and black **peppercorns** (and a pepper mill).
6 **Herbs** such as rosemary, bay leaf, sage, and thyme, though these can be found about the place if you're lucky and it has a garden.

BRUNCH
MERGUEZ SAUSAGES, SPICED POTATOES, AND EGGS

SERVES 8
PREP 20 MINUTES
COOK ABOUT 1 HOUR

FOR THE SPICE MIX

3 tablespoons cumin seeds

3 tablespoons coriander seeds

1 tablespoon black peppercorns

1 cinnamon stick

½ teaspoon yellow or black mustard seeds

1 teaspoon dried red pepper flakes

1 teaspoon turmeric

1 tablespoon smoked paprika

½ teaspoon freshly ground nutmeg

FOR THE BRUNCH ITSELF

1¼ pounds new potatoes, halved if large

16 merguez sausages (the thinner sort)

5 tablespoons olive oil

2 large onions, halved and sliced

2 red bell peppers, seeded and cut into strips

5 tomatoes, each cut into six

3½ ounces spinach, washed and drained well

8 very, very fresh eggs (optional)

small handful of chopped parsley

a little smoked paprika (optional)

harissa paste, to serve (optional)

BLENDING SMALL BATCHES OF SPICES AT HOME allows you subtly to adjust the balance until it suits your taste. Cloves, allspice, cayenne, or saffron (all in judicious amounts), or fennel seeds, mace, or ginger, would be worthwhile additions to the basic mix as written. If you start by buying the whole spices from a good Asian store with a fast turnover, then toast and grind, the results will beat most store-bought blends. Not to mention the convenience of using one ready-to-go jar, as opposed to rootling around in the back of the cupboard for ten different spices halfway through a recipe (just me?).

Make your spice mix a few days beforehand and keep in a lidded jar for up to three months. Note its name and expiration date on a label. You won't have trouble using it up: dust over fish, chicken, or vegetables before roasting, stir into olive oil to finish a lentil soup, or spoon onto softened onions and garlic at the start of a tagine.

You could easily use a store-bought spice mix for this recipe instead of making your own. It needs to match the flavors of the sausages and complement the vegetables, so try a *ras el hanout*, translated as "top of the shop." Each spice merchant makes his own secret North African blend with his very best spices, hence the name.

Here, crisp, spiced potatoes accompany merguez sausages, stained with smoked paprika and a panful of colorful vegetables. To finish it all off, top with a poached (or fried, if you prefer) egg and a little chopped parsley. Breakfast or brunch fodder for champions.

Start by making your spice mix. Toast the spices, except for the turmeric, paprika, and nutmeg, gently in a dry skillet, stirring them to toast evenly. Remove from the heat when they look darker—but not burned—and smell fragrant. Add the turmeric, paprika, and nutmeg and either pound everything together in a mortar and pestle, or grind in a spice mill or a coffee grinder (permanently designated to grinding spices, rather than beans, for the sake of your morning coffee). Store in a lidded jar, label, and use within 3 months.

When you are ready to cook brunch, preheat the oven to 425°F. Parboil the potatoes in plenty of simmering water and a pinch of salt

CONTINUED ...

for 15 minutes or so, until just tender to the point of a knife. Drain in a colander.

Meanwhile, quickly brown the sausages with 2 tablespoons of the oil, in two batches if necessary, in a large skillet set over high heat. Once seared, remove to a roasting pan with a slotted spoon, leaving the paprika-stained oil in the pan.

Add the potatoes to the sausages in their roasting pan, with the remaining oil. Tumble around to coat everything in oil, then scatter with 1½ tablespoons of the spice mix. Roast for 15 to 20 minutes, until the potatoes are turning golden. Turn the oven off with the pan still inside and leave the door ajar. Add a stack of plates to warm.

Get a deep skillet, full of water, coming up to a boil if you intend on poaching eggs.

Throw the onions and peppers into the skillet with the oil from the sausages and 1 teaspoon of spice mix. Fry over medium heat, stirring often, for about 10 minutes, until all is softened and beginning to brown. Now add the tomatoes and cook for another 10 minutes, stirring and adding a splash of water if anything sticks. Fold in the spinach and remove from the heat. Season well and keep warm.

When the poached egg water is simmering gently —that's lots of gentle bubbles but no violent boiling—submerge the eggs, whole and in their shells, beneath the water for 20 seconds. Remove with a slotted spoon. One by one, carefully crack each egg into a small cup. Hold the cup as near to the water's surface as possible and gently slide the egg in, causing as little disturbance as possible. Repeat with the other eggs. Let cook at this very gentle simmer for 3 to 4 minutes, until the whites are set but the yolks are still liquid. You may need gently to encourage them to lift off the bottom if they sink downward. Use a slotted spoon to remove the eggs to a plate, first allowing any excess water to drain away.

Serve a small pile of potatoes and two sausages with a spoonful of the vegetable mixture. Top each warmed plateful with an egg and a scattering of parsley. You could add a rust-red dusting of smoked paprika, if you have some handy. Offer harissa on the side for those who like the heat.

A NOTE ON POACHING EGGS

I've had too many conversations about perfect egg poaching being an impossible feat. Not so. If you follow the method above, you will cook the perfect poached egg with absolutely no swirling or—my absolute hate—dire, vinegary water. The most important point is this: your eggs must be spankingly fresh for the whites to hold together. If they are more than a few days old, scramble or boil them or make meringues instead. The reason I add whole eggs to the simmering water before cracking them open is to warm the whites through and begin the setting process. This helps keep it together once cracked, instead of floating away in a sea of albumen lace.

If you go gently at the final stage and barely plop the cracked egg into the boiling water, it should hold like a dream, and perfect poached eggs will be yours.

LUNCH
YOUNG BEETS IN PARCELS

THIS IS HARDLY A FORMAL RECIPE. THINK OF IT AS A SUGGESTION and adjust the quantities to your taste, adding more or no garlic, a different herb, a sweet sherry vinegar . . .

Any available beets should be small and tender this early in the season. Chop any larger ones into wedges. You'll also need parchment paper and kitchen string, or foil, for wrapping.

Preheat the oven to 375°F. Slice smaller beets in half, or quarter if large.

Cut out 8 squares of foil or parchment paper; each needs to be about 8 inches square. Scrunch the paper up a little to stop liquid running straight out of it and, in the center of each square, sit a pile of beets, a bruised garlic clove, a couple of sprigs of thyme, a scattering of salt and pepper, a splash of balsamic, and the same of olive oil.

Fold and wrap the excess paper in, as if you were wrapping a present. Tie in place with kitchen string. If you use foil, no string will be needed, you can just crush the edges into place.

Bake for 1 hour, until the beets are glazed, tender, and concentrated in flavor. Take the parcels to the table and let everybody unwrap their own.

SERVES 8 AS A SIDE DISH
PREP 20 MINUTES
COOK 1 HOUR

12-16 young multicolored beets,
   scrubbed, trimmed
8 fat garlic cloves, bruised, but
   left whole and in their skins
handful of sprigs of thyme
good balsamic vinegar
extra-virgin olive oil

LUNCH
PORCHETTA STUFFED WITH FARRO

PORCHETTA, YES, BUT DONE MY WAY, with a garlic-scented farro stuffing that intensifies as the pork roasts to tenderness. The extra grain cooked makes the base for a warm salad to accompany the joint. You can find newly trendy farro in delis with a good stock of Italian ingredients, or in health food stores. Substitute with spelt or barley, which have similar nutty tones but slightly less texture once cooked.

Toast the pine nuts in a dry skillet, shaking often until golden. Combine the garlic, rosemary, and sage in a bowl and set aside.

In a large casserole or pan, soften the onions in the olive oil for 10 minutes, until coloring at the edges. Add half the chopped garlic and herb mixture and cook for a few seconds, then stir in the farro and stock. Bring to a boil, cover, and simmer, lid askew, for 30 minutes, or until the liquid has been absorbed and the grains are tender, but not insipidly so. Stir in the pine nuts and cool slightly.

Meanwhile, preheat your oven to its highest setting. To make it easier to tie the pork after stuffing it, cut 5 lengths of kitchen string—each about 16 inches if you're measuring—and lay them out in parallel, each evenly spaced below the other. Lay the pork on top, skin-side down. Make a few more shallow cuts in the flesh to increase its surface area, then smear the remaining garlic and herbs all over with plenty of salt and pepper. Spoon a scant quarter of the farro down the middle, and then bring the sides up around it and roll as tightly as you can. Tie the string tightly around to keep the shape.

Now anoint the surface with about 2 tablespoons olive oil and rub liberally with salt to help the skin crisp as it roasts. Lay the celery, carrot, and shallots in a sturdy roasting pan, sit the pork on top, and add the wine with 1¼ cups water. Slide into the center of the oven and immediately reduce the heat to 350°F. Roast for 3 to 3½ hours, until deeply golden, crisp, and beginning to bubble.

Rest the pork in the pan for a few minutes. Snip through the string and carve into slices; you might find it easier to remove the crisp skin in one go first. Place the pan over low heat, scraping to remove any good caramelized bits and adding a dash more water to make a light gravy. Strain into a pitcher. Serve the pork with the Farro and Green Bean Salad (see page 54) and the warm pan juices.

SERVES 8
PREP 30 MINUTES
COOK 3¾ TO 4¼ HOURS

FOR THE FARRO STUFFING (WITH LEFTOVER FOR THE SALAD, SEE PAGE 54)
¾ cup pine nuts
4 fat garlic cloves, minced
leaves from 4 sprigs of rosemary, chopped
6 large sage leaves, chopped
2 large red onions, chopped
3 tablespoons olive oil, plus more for the crackling
1 pound 2 ounces farro or spelt
4 cups light vegetable stock or water

FOR THE PORK
6½ pounds pork shoulder, boned, butterflied, and skin scored
2 celery stalks, roughly chopped
1 carrot, roughly chopped
2 banana shallots, halved, or 1 onion, sliced (no need to peel)
generous 1 cup white wine

LUNCH
FARRO AND GREEN BEAN SALAD

SERVES 8 GENEROUSLY
PREP 20 MINUTES
COOK 5 MINUTES

FOR THE DRESSING
5 tablespoons extra-virgin olive
  oil, or to taste
2 tablespoons red wine vinegar,
  or to taste
pinch of sugar, or to taste

FOR THE SALAD
cooked farro base from
  Porchetta Stuffed with Farro
  (see page 53)
1 pound 2 ounces green beans,
  trimmed
7 ounces young carrots,
  scrubbed, sliced only if larger
  than a little finger
2 handfuls of mixed summer
  herbs, minced
generous ¾ cup ricotta salata,
  roughly crumbled

THIS WILL MAKE A LOVELY ACCOMPANIMENT TO THE PORK but, if you have any vegetarians in your party, a warm salad makes an excellent main course to compensate for the lack of pork and will still be very good cold the following day. I've assumed you'll be making both, but that is rather arrogant of me, so, if you'd like to rebel and make the salad without making the pork, follow the directions in the Porchetta Stuffed with Farro recipe (see page 53) with the odd adjustment. Soften the onions but add slightly less of the chopped garlic and herbs. Use only 14 ounces farro or spelt and 3⅓ cups stock or water, then simmer until cooked as in the main recipe. Add the toasted pine nuts once cooked.

If you can't get ricotta salata, use a firm but fresh-tasting, salty cheese; try a young pecorino or even a crumbled cheddar. For the mixed herbs, I used snipped chives and chive flowers, with mint, basil, and chervil, but any soft spring herbs you like will be lovely here; the key is bounty so use a free hand.

Combine the dressing ingredients with salt and pepper. Taste and adjust with more oil, vinegar, or sugar until it tastes good to you.

If the cooked farro is cold, cover and warm through in a low oven.

Steam the beans and carrots over boiling water for about 4 minutes, until just tender. Add to the farro with the herbs, stir briefly, then douse with the dressing. Fold through the ricotta. Taste and add more seasoning if needed. Serve warm.

Wild Swimming

What better after a weekend walk and a picnic than to happen upon some halcyon pond, pool, beach, or looping river bend to laze about in? The best are tranquil spots, away from the maddening crowds, but you might have to work hard at discovering them. Keep the splashing to a minimum and you're likely to see all sorts of wildlife, both above and below the water.

PONDS AND SMALL LAKES

Are invariably warmer than the sea; in the later days of a good summer, it's not unusual for the water temperature to reach a balmy 68°F. At other times of the year—and for sea swimming—a wetsuit might be an idea.

WATERFALL AND PLUNGE POOLS

Fed by a waterfall or, in less-spectacular cases, a stream, plunge pools or swimming holes are usually icy cool and, hopefully, deep enough to dive into. (It is ALWAYS absolutely essential to check this before jumping in!)

Enormous coastal tidal pools, left for a few hours at low tide, also make ideal saltwater swimming pools, and there will be a great deal to look at below the surface and in surrounding, smaller, tidal pools.

COASTLINES

For the brave swimmer, undeterred by cold, be fearless about exploring the plethora of sandy beaches, rocky outcrops, secret bays, islands, arches, and caves there are to discover year round. Take a snorkel; you'll be amazed at what you can see. Get to know the stretch of coastline you're exploring, including the tide times and any areas with high currents or unsuitable ground that should be avoided.

SLOW-MOVING RIVERS

Meandering rivers, housing bends, and loops with very little current often provide the perfect conditions for a swim. The water will be cold where the sun's rays can't reach, so float on the surface or prepare for cold legs!

SAFETY ADVICE

Getting overly "health and safety" takes away from the pleasure of wild swimming so, assuming you are a strong swimmer, don't trespass and use your common sense. However, there are a few rules to stick to, especially when venturing into a location you don't know well:

Never swim where fishermen are. Their potential wrath at the disturbance should be enough to put you off, but a barbed hook through the eye would be so much worse.

When assessing a river for swimming potential, look for fords and firm, sloping banks so that you can climb out easily. Wear shoes to protect your feet and ease in slowly, making sure you're happy with the depth.

If you are worried about the cleanliness of the water, contact your local environment agency beforehand for information.

Our coastline houses a veritable treasure chest of secluded bays and beaches, but the ocean can be brutal so play it safe and always leave yourself a generous amount of leeway. Fishermen and wise locals should know what's what, so ask them about tides, incoming weather, and known danger spots. Be aware if rising tides could strand you on a section of beach or rock.

3 of my favorite
WILD SWIMMING SPOTS

Growing up as we did in the sleepy English countryside and not too far from the sea, jumping in local lakes, rivers, and coastal waters was a common summer activity for my brother and me. The flora and fauna in Britain are generally pretty safe, so there wasn't much to worry about back then . . . obviously, you'll have to use your judgment and local knowledge when assessing potential waters. If you do ever find yourself in the British Isles in the warmer months, you could do worse than seeking out one of my favorite places.

TREYARNON BAY beach on the north coast of Cornwall, west England, reveals spectacular—and very large—rock pools at low tide. They are perfect for swimming and paddling, though wetsuit boots or jelly shoes with a good grip are recommended to protect soft feet from the rocks and any sharp underwater creatures.

The stunning INGRAM VALLEY houses the River Breamish and runs through Northumberland National Park in the north of England. The river itself is suitable for a paddle and a splash-about in warm weather, but follow the road to the end of the valley and walk up the marked path for a couple of miles, to reach Linhope Spout, a particularly beautiful waterfall with a plunge pool below for swimming in.

Local to my family home is THE ANCHOR INN, just outside Barcombe in East Sussex in the south of England. From there, it's well known that you can hire rowing boats to amble along the Ouse toward a pretty dam. Most give up and turn around before they get to the end, but it's worth the inevitable arm ache for a secluded dip. There are plenty of rope swings and swimworthy river bends to amuse on a shorter trip though. Just be prepared to dodge shrieking, dive-bombing teenagers in high summer.

LUNCH
APRICOT AND FIRST RASPBERRY LATTICE TART

SERVES 8, WITH ICE CREAM
PREP 30 MINUTES, PLUS
  CHILLING TIME
COOK 1 HOUR

a little all-purpose flour, for
  rolling
1 pound 2 ounces basic pie dough
  (slightly sweetened, ideally)
3 tablespoons ground almonds
4 tablespoons brown sugar
7 ripe apricots, halved and pitted
1²/₃ cups raspberries
whole milk, to glaze
2 tablespoons raw brown sugar
  (optional)

A DESSERT TO CELEBRATE THOSE TENTATIVE EARLY RASPBERRIES. If none are to be found, buy them frozen instead and defrost before using.

The filling isn't overly saccharine, so this rustic, juicy mix benefits from a good and short basic pie dough recipe with a touch of sweetness. You might want to halve the pastry component for the Chicken and Wild Mushroom Pies (see page 124), stirring in 2 tablespoons confectioners' sugar before adding the water. An all-butter store-bought pastry would do perfectly well, too.

First dusting with a very little flour, roll the pie dough out into a large circle, about ⅛ inch thick. Line an 8-inch pie dish, being careful not to stretch the dough or it will shrink back on cooking. Trim the edges with scissors, leaving a good ½-inch overhang. Let chill for at least 30 minutes or up to a few hours. Preheat the oven to 350°F.

Now trim the excess pie dough flush with the pan, using a sharp knife. Scatter the base with the ground almonds and 1 tablespoon of the brown sugar. Lay the apricots on top, cut-sides up, and scatter with half the remaining brown sugar. Sprinkle the raspberries on and around, finishing with the last of the brown sugar.

Reroll the remaining pie dough and cut into strips of about 10 inches. Lay these across the top in a lattice pattern, sticking them into place with a drop of milk. Brush the lattice with milk and, if you like, dredge with raw brown sugar to create a crunchy sugar top.

Bake for about 1 hour, covering loosely with foil if the pastry lattice browns too quickly. Serve warm, straight from the pan with the frozen yogurt, if you have made it. Otherwise, cream, crème fraîche, or vanilla ice cream would make lovely substitutes.

FROZEN YOGURT

IF YOU HAVE AN ICE-CREAM MACHINE, you can get away with using a good, whole milk yogurt but, if you make this by hand (almost certainly the case in a vacation house), the density of a whole Greek yogurt is essential for a really creamy result.

Stir the yogurt, sugar, lemon juice, and vanilla until the sugar dissolves. Freeze for an hour. If you have an ice-cream maker, freeze the mixture according to the manufacturer's directions.

All is not lost, however, if you need to make this by hand. Freeze the chilled mixture in a sturdy, shallow container for 1 hour, then whisk vigorously with a balloon whisk to break up and mix in any ice crystals at the edges. Return to the freezer for 30 minutes, then whisk again, repeating this every ½ hour for another 2 hours. Let firm up in the freezer for 1 to 2 hours. This is best soon after making but will keep, covered, for a couple of weeks. In the latter case, soften in the refrigerator until scoopable before serving.

**SERVES 8 AS AN
  ACCOMPANIMENT**
PREP 10 MINUTES, PLUS 1 HOUR
  CHILLING
FREEZE 20 TO 30 MINUTES IN AN
  ICE-CREAM MACHINE; ABOUT
  3½ HOURS BY HAND.

generous 3 cups thick, Greek-
  style yogurt (not reduced fat),
  chilled
scant ²⁄₃ cup superfine sugar
2 teaspoons lemon juice
½ vanilla bean, seeds scraped
  out, or 1 teaspoon vanilla
  extract

SUPPER
GALETTES DE BLÉ NOIR

SUCH A LYRICAL NAME WHEN COMPARED WITH THEIR ENGLISH TRANSLATION: buckwheat crêpes, Breton-style. This batter is a dream for making ahead as it needs to settle and swell overnight before making the crêpes. Use the largest skillet or crêpe pan you can get your hands on. A cast-iron, flat griddle will produce the ultimate in galettes, but improvising is just fine.

This filling is traditional and simple; lovely for brunch or lunch as well as an early supper. Using egg yolks only is a solution to the egg white taking too long to cook and ruining the timings. A poached or fried egg, added before folding the crêpe, would solve that problem. Distinctive, toasty buckwheat is found in blinis, so it follows that smoked salmon, crème fraîche, or cream cheese and dill is welcome in a crisp-edged galette. Or try sautéed leeks, ham, and gruyère or just ham and gruyère with no egg yolk; buttered spinach, nutmeg, and ricotta; buttered spinach and gruyère; jam and butter; fruit compote and ice cream; melted chocolate, banana, and ice cream . . .

MAKES 8
PREP 30 MINUTES, PLUS
    OVERNIGHT CHILLING TIME
COOK 15 MINUTES

FOR THE GALETTES
about 7 tablespoons butter, softened
1 egg, beaten
1¼ cups whole milk
½ teaspoon salt
scant 1 cup buckwheat flour
scant ½ cup all-purpose flour

FOR THE FILLING
8 thin slices of ham
1 cups finely grated gruyère cheese
8 egg yolks

Melt 2 tablespoons of the butter and let cool slightly. Using electric beaters, whisk the melted butter with the egg, ⅔ cup of the milk, the salt, and 1¼ cups cool water in a large bowl. Gradually whisk in the flours to form a smooth batter. Keep whisking for a couple of minutes. You can do this by hand, first mixing the batter with a balloon whisk, then using the outstretched fingers of one hand to stir around, lift up, and slap the batter down in a smooth motion. Continue for about 4 minutes. Either way, the batter should be smooth and elastic. Cover and chill overnight, or for up to 24 hours. Stir the remaining milk into the batter with ⅔ cup water. The consistency should be somewhere close to light cream.

Heat a very large, nonstick skillet or crêpe pan over medium heat. Using paper towels, brush the surface with butter. Pour a small ladleful of batter into the pan, swirling it to cover the bottom thinly. Cook for about 2 minutes, until golden beneath and lacy at the edges. Use a spatula to flip over and cook for a minute more. Working swiftly, scrape with a smear of butter, a slice of ham, and a nest of gruyère. Drop an egg yolk into the cheese and twist some pepper over. Cook until the yolk is setting at the edges. Flip in the edges to make a parcel and slide onto a plate. Repeat with the remaining ingredients to make 8 folded galettes.

SUPPER
KOHLRABI SALAD

KOHLRABI, WHICH RESEMBLE FANTASTICAL GREEN OR PURPLE SPACESHIPS depending on the variety, are much underused. Their crisp flesh—akin to turnips but more like broccoli stalks in flavor—roasts, fries, stir-fries, and braises well but can also be stuffed or combined with celery root in a mustardy rémoulade. Kohlrabi greens wilt down as well as any cabbage. I also think the bulb itself is an absolute winner in Thai and Vietnamese salads, shredded and generously dressed, with seared beef—thinly sliced—crushed peanuts, chilies, and plenty of mint or Thai basil. Look for small kohlrabi, each no bigger than about 9 inches in circumference. At this time of year, the early, homegrown examples will be small with tender flesh, suited to slicing into rounds and eating uncooked. Delightful as it is, a Thai influence would feel incongruous in this menu, so I have gone with a simple raw salad (with a resolutely European influence) to accompany the warm galettes.

Use a mandolin or, far more time-consuming, a sharp knife to very finely slice the kohlrabi (a food processor slices a little too thickly for this job). Failing that, coarsely grate the flesh, wringing it out in a dish towel to get rid of any excess water.

Dress the kohlrabi, scallions, and chives generously with lime juice and olive oil, season, and set aside for about 5 minutes. Tumble the watercress through just before serving.

SERVES 8 AS A SIDE DISH
PREP 15 MINUTES

1 pound 2 ounces young, small
   kohlrabi, peeled
4 scallions, very finely sliced
½ bunch of chives, finely snipped
good squeeze of lime juice
extra-virgin olive oil
2 handfuls of watercress, large
   stems removed

A NOTE ON SLICING AND SHREDDING

The most unlikely vegetables can make excellent salad subjects if they are treated right. Consider a vegetable like a kohlrabi or celery root; shaving whisper-thin slices or toothsome shreds gives them such interesting and versatile texture, rendering raw flesh—that would perhaps be too dense to tackle in large pieces—delicate and easy to eat. There are two pieces of equipment I find invaluable when making salads. First, a small mandolin (such is my paranoia that I use the hand guard without fail)—nothing fancy, mine is just a cheap and light Japanese model from a local kitchen store—to make light work of slicing vegetables and fruit paper thin. The other recommendation is a little shredder (officially known as a kiwi), resembling a swivel vegetable peeler with a serrated blade. You can pick one up very cheaply from any Vietnamese or Thai food store to make light work of green papaya and the like for Southeast Asian salads.

LAID-BACK COUNTRY WEDDING FOR 20

With enough cake for many more . . .

SWEET PEPPER SAUSAGE ROLLS | HOME-SMOKED TROUT WITH CAPER MAYONNAISE | **SQUASH AND MANOURI SALAD** | *Summer grilled roast of lamb* | GRILLED ARTICHOKES WITH ALMONDS | FOCACCIA BOARDS | *Splendid strawberry and vanilla cake* | Drinks station: basil limeade; raspberry crush; elderflower vodka

Catering for weddings instills fear into the hearts of even seasoned chefs. This is a menu for a charming and relaxed outdoor gathering, tiny by wedding standards (though everything except the cake can easily be doubled).

Slices of warm sausage roll, each enclosing an herbed pepper compote, will temper raging appetites before lunch. If an appetizer is called for, the smoked trout is eminently suitable, but the rest—the salad, lamb, artichokes, and bread —can all be laid out, family-style, on a long table. Divide each between more than one serving dish and set them down the center of the table, making sure to provide plenty of serving spoons.

The table only needs humble decoration. Summer flowers in multiple jam jars and small bottles look graceful and winsome. Fill two or three small tin baths, the kind found in antique stores and as quirky plant containers, with ice and water. Tuck them in the shade near to the table, evenly spaced along its length. They will serve as white wine, beer, and champagne coolers. If you intend on returning any unopened bottles, keep them in the refrigerator rather than submerged in water, or the labels will peel off. An independent table serves as a drinks station for freshly made coolers and crushes.

In an attempt to free up the oven for sausage rolls and warming bread, the lamb is cooked via a slightly alternate method, first searing on a hot grill, then having a short blast in a hot oven, then being wrapped in foil and a thick blanket, where it sits, slowly cooking in the residual heat, for three to four hours. This is such a boon when cooking for large numbers; a few minutes extra resting won't hurt and the work has been done in advance.

The cake waits for dancers. It will sit patiently, in a very cool room, ready to be brought out and cut later in the day, once the music has started and a flood of extra guests has arrived.

SWEET PEPPER SAUSAGE ROLLS

THESE ARE RUSTIC SAUSAGE ROLLS, so don't expect them to look too pretty when they come out of the oven; their beauty is in their imperfection. Roasted sweet peppers and handfuls of herbs are baked into the rolls, providing a sort of integrated relish. Only better. Serve them from wooden boards as people mill about, with a glass of champagne or a beer and plenty of napkins.

Preheat the oven to 425°F. Lay the pepper halves in a single layer across two baking sheets, skin-sides up. Drizzle with a little olive oil, to help the skins to blister. Roast for about 40 minutes, until truly blackened and soft. Tip the hot peppers into a bowl and cover it with a plate to keep the steam in. Set aside to cool until you can handle the peppers comfortably.

Peel the skins off and throw them away. Slice the pepper flesh into rough strips and combine it with the chopped herbs, balsamic vinegar, and a little salt and pepper. You can make this up to about four days in advance. Keep the peppers chilled. Reduce the oven temperature to 375°F.

Combine the egg yolk and milk in a cup to make an egg wash. Divide the pastry in half. On a lightly floured counter, roll the first block out to form a long, thin rectangle. Trim the edges to form a neat rectangle of about 6 by 16 inches.

Divide the sausage meat in half. Form the first half into a long sausage, the same length as the pastry rectangle. Dust with flour and lay it over the pastry, about 1½ inches from one edge. Flatten the sausage slightly and top with half the roast pepper mixture. Roll the pastry around the sausage, sealing the edges with egg wash. Repeat with the remaining pastry and filling ingredients. Transfer both rolls to a large baking sheet. At this stage the rolls can be refrigerated overnight, just bring them up to room temperature before baking.

Brush both rolls generously with egg wash and diagonally slash the tops a few times, down the length of the roll. Bake for 35 to 40 minutes, until golden brown and well-risen. Slice the rolls into chunky pieces with a sharp, serrated knife and serve warm.

**MAKES 2 LARGE ROLLS; EACH
CUTS INTO 15 TO 20 PIECES**
PREP 50 MINUTES
COOK ABOUT 1¼ HOURS

7 mixed red, yellow, or
    orange bell peppers, halved
olive oil
small handful each of basil,
    parsley, and thyme, chopped
2 tablespoons good-quality
    balsamic vinegar
1 egg yolk
2 tablespoons milk
1 pound 2 ounces all-butter puff
    pastry
a little all-purpose flour, to dust
2¼ pounds best-quality
    sausages, casings removed

HOME-SMOKED TROUT WITH CAPER MAYONNAISE

I STARTED WORK ON THIS CELEBRATORY RECIPE BY COOKING IT INDOORS, using a wok as a mini hot-smoker on the stove. As the testing went on, however, I remembered why I rarely smoke meat and fish in this way any more: your house, drapes, clothes, and hair will reek like a bonfire and only after a good few hours of airing the place—and at least one shower—will it begin to subside. Subsequently, the method I give below is for using a lidded grill as an outdoor hot-smoker. If you would like to explore the subject further, I give directions on how to make your own hot-smoker on page 69.

The brief brining has several benefits. It will season, further preserve, and, due to the sugar, tenderize the fish. After rinsing, the residual brine also hardens slightly when left to dry out, forming a protective surface to support the fish as it smokes and cooks.

All this smoking business does seem like a bother, but I promise you it is a fun process once you get the hang of it; the results are truly excellent and well worth the trouble. But if the point of the thing eludes you, simply use store-bought hot-smoked trout. You'll need about eight large trout fillets to serve this crowd with buttered squares of rye bread, watercress, and dabs of caper mayonnaise. Ethereal fennel flowers bloom abundantly in these summer months. If you have a ready supply, add a few as (edible) finishing touches; their anise perfume complements trout beautifully.

Make the mayonnaise in advance. Using a food processor or a strong arm, briefly blend or whisk the egg yolks to break them down. Start adding the olive oil (reserving the extra 3 tablespoons) drop by drop—no faster—with the blades (or whisk) whirring. As the oil is incorporated you may increase the drops to a very thin trickle, but don't try to add it too fast or it could well split. Now start adding the canola or peanut oil, again gradually increasing the trickle as more is added, until the mayonnaise is thick and shiny and all the oil has been absorbed.

If the mixture splits, gradually whisk another egg yolk into the split mixture to bring it back and continue adding the oil as before, going more slowly this time.

Stir in the mustard and 3 tablespoons of the chopped capers. Chop 2 tablespoons of the parsley and stir this in too. Adjust the consistency

CONTINUED . . .

ENOUGH FOR 20 AS A SUBSTANTIAL APPETIZER OR PART OF A BUFFET
PREP 30 MINUTES, PLUS BRINING
COOK 25 TO 55 MINUTES

FOR THE CAPER MAYONNAISE
3 large egg yolks
$^2/_3$ cup mild-flavored olive oil, plus 3 tablespoons more
$1^1/_4$ cups canola or peanut oil
2 teaspoons Dijon mustard
5 tablespoons salted capers, rinsed and chopped
2 small bunches of parsley
lemon juice, to taste

and brighten the seasoning with a squeeze of lemon juice. Cover and chill for up to 4 days.

Now to the trout. They may be smoked up to 5 days in advance, then wrapped and chilled until needed.

Make the brine by mixing the salt, sugar, and pepper with 2 cups cool water. A lidded plastic container, big enough to hold the fish, is ideal for this. Submerge the cleaned and scaled trout in the brine for 1 hour.

Rinse very briefly under cold running water—just to get rid of the excess salt—and dry the fish by patting them with paper towels. Meanwhile, light the grill coals and let them burn down until gray and glowing. No visible flame should remain. Dampen your sawdust or woodchips slightly then drop them in a border around the outer ring of coals. Scrunch up a double sheet of foil, then cut or tear it to form a cup. Sit it in the center of the coals, leaving the wood border exposed. Pour about ½ cup water into this foil cup and sit the metal grate above.

Lay the trout on the grate and close the lid. Smoke for 40 to 50 minutes, but check after a mere 20 as both fish size and the heat from grill to grill will vary greatly. As soon as the flesh near the backbone flakes easily to the point of a knife, but remains slightly translucent and moist, remove the fish, grate and all. The skin will be burnished and golden around the belly. The trout will continue to cook a little more as they cool. Once cooled, they may be refrigerated or used immediately.

When lunchtime rolls around, lay your magnificent fish on large platters, ready to be skinned and flaked to order. Just before serving, heat the reserved 3 tablespoons olive oil in a skillet over medium heat. Fry the reserved capers and parsley until sizzling and crisp.

Spoon the hot caper and parsley mixture over and around the trout. Bowlfuls of caper mayonnaise, piles of watercress, buttered rye bread slices, and those optional but decorative fennel flowers should all be offered alongside the trout.

FOR THE FISH

4 tablespoons sea salt
4 tablespoons brown sugar
1 tablespoon cracked black pepper
4 large, fresh rainbow or brown trout, about 1 pound to 1 pound 2 ounces each, cleaned

TO SMOKE THE FISH

lidded grill, with coals and a metal grate
2 large handfuls of oak or apple woodchips
2 sheets of sturdy foil

TO SERVE

2 handfuls of watercress, washed and dried
20 large or 40 small slices of buttered rye bread
10 fennel flower heads (optional)

BUILDING
a home smoker

Hot home smoking, or "barbecue," is relatively easy to achieve at home; all you need is a lidded grill of sorts—whether store-bought or improvised—and a source of smoke.

By slowly grilling the food (be that fish, meat, poultry, or vegetables) over smoldering, damp wood in a closed chamber, it will gently smoke as it cooks. Large, fatty cuts of meat are suited to home smoking, as it's a good treatment for a long cooking time and a lowish heat, very like firepit cooking (see pages 135–141). The fat will slowly render out, leaving extremely tender and succulent meat. In fact, the home smoker and the firepit have much in common; one simply happens to be above ground and the other below.

Choose a sweet wood as your smoke source. Cherry, apple, and pear are all ideal, as is oak, though it creates a stronger smoke. Hickory chips or chunks are very strong, so use them sparingly or mix with other woods. Soak the wood in water for a few hours (a minimum of one hour is key); the more saturated the wood, the more smoke it will produce. You'll need about four logs for a standard, Weber-style lidded grill, or a couple of good double handfuls of wood chunks or chips (these should also be soaked and drained before use). I prefer logs because they smolder far longer than chips or chunks, but any type will do.

Light the grill and wait for the coals to burn down to an ashen gray-white. Have the metal grate set as high up as possible; you don't want it too close to the coals or the food will scorch. Use tongs to scrape some of the coals aside, then throw the soaked wood into the center. Rake some coals back on top of the wood. You should have created

a good supply of smoke. Fit the metal grate in place, set your chosen food on top, and close the lid.

Cook fish until it gives to the touch. It will be firm, but should flake reluctantly. (For safe poultry and meat temperatures, see the chart on page 12 and use a meat thermometer to check.) Large joints will need a long cooking time; small cuts should be checked after thirty minutes and monitored from that time onward. Cooking times will depend entirely on the heat of your grill. You will become an expert hot smoker with just a little practice, but it does take a couple of tries to get the knack.

It is possible to create a cold smoker by using far, far fewer coals—only a handful really—and smoking the food (this is particularly good for fish) for three to four hours. In this case, the temperature inside the grill should hover around 100°F. You may first want to brine meat or fish, or at least leave it uncovered in the refrigerator overnight, to form a tacky, hardened surface, known as a pellicule, which will protect the flesh below.

You can also use rosemary, thyme, or bay branches to create smoke, just as you would with soaked wood logs, chunks, or chips. Dampen the leaves, then throw them over ashen-gray coals to create a smoke that will imbue the food with a beautiful herbal taste.

SQUASH AND MANOURI SALAD

YOU MAY HAVE GLEANED, FROM A QUICK FLICK THROUGH THESE PAGES, that I am fond of dense-fleshed squash, especially when roasted. To defend my amour, it is dictated by head as well as heart. A trayful of caramelized squash is one of the easiest, and most versatile, solutions to feeding a crowd well, from soups, stews, and curries, to salads both warm and cool.

Greek delis are the most reliable source of manouri cheese, a fresh, semisoft white cheese, not dissimilar to a soft feta but with none of its saltiness. With a lemon and dill dressing and a pinch of dried red pepper flakes, it tastes fantastic. You could substitute feta that you have first soaked in water for a few hours, or even better, one of the great array of manouri-like cheeses sold in good Middle Eastern food stores. Verjuice I love. Deeply. It is pressed from unripe grapes and makes a beautiful dressing, but don't panic if you can't find it; simply use lemon juice and honey instead.

Preheat the oven to 400°F. Slice the peeled squash in half, digging out the seeds with a spoon. Cut each half into half-moons. Toss with the olive oil, season generously, and roast on two large, lined baking sheets for about 50 minutes, until dark at the edges and tender. Turn carefully with a spatula halfway. Let cool. This can be done 2 days beforehand and the squash kept chilled and covered. Return to room temperature before using.

To make the dressing, whisk the extra-virgin olive oil and verjuice together (or replace the verjuice with honey and the juice of 1 lemon). Add the red pepper flakes, fennel seeds, and lemon zest. Stir in half the chopped dill. Taste, season, and taste again, then add more verjuice or honey and lemon juice, if you want. Make this up to 3 days in advance and keep it chilled, but only add the dill just before using.

To serve, divide the remaining dill, the arugula, olives, and roast squash between two or three serving bowls. Whisk the dressing well and spoon a little over each bowlful. Toss gently to coat the arugula leaves lightly. Now add the manouri, gently distributing it among the salad ingredients so as not to break the cheese up too much. Spoon the remaining dressing evenly over each bowlful, sprinkle with a little extra dried red pepper flakes, if you wish, and sea salt (remember that the cheese contains no salt at all). Serve soon after.

ENOUGH FOR 20 AS A SIDE DISH, OR 10 AS A MAIN COURSE
PREP 20 MINUTES
COOK 45 MINUTES

FOR THE SALAD
2 large coquina or butternut squash, peeled
5 tablespoons olive oil
3 large handfuls of arugula
2 handfuls of large green olives in oil, drained and pitted
1¼ pounds manouri cheese, broken into rough pieces

FOR THE DRESSING
¾ cup extra-virgin olive oil
5 tablespoons verjuice, or 2 tablespoons liquid honey, to taste
2 unwaxed lemons, finely grated zest of both and juice to taste (optional)
½ teaspoon dried red pepper flakes, plus a pinch to serve
2 teaspoons fennel seeds, lightly crushed
large bunch of dill, chopped

SUMMER GRILLED ROAST OF LAMB

THIS MAY SEEM A STRANGE RECIPE AT FIRST GLANCE, BUT I DEVELOPED IT from an old French technique I read about, to free up the oven and do away with any notions of tending a grill for hours. The lamb is first seared, then put in a hot oven, then left to finish cooking wrapped in a thick blanket. A large griddle pan or skillet will be enough for searing the lamb if you don't have the wherewithal to grill it. The herb paste is a gutsy cousin to salsa verde. Half is rubbed over the lamb before searing; half is combined with good olive oil and served alongside the cooked meat.

ENOUGH FOR 20 AS PART OF THIS MENU; EASILY HALVED TO SERVE 6 TO 8 AS A MAIN COURSE
PREP 20 MINUTES
COOK 45 MINUTES, PLUS 3 TO 4 HOURS "RESTING"

FOR THE HERB PASTE
large bunch of chervil, roughly chopped
large bunch of parsley, roughly chopped
large bunch of basil, roughly chopped
10 fat garlic cloves, peeled
small can of anchovies in olive oil, drained
10-ounce jar sundried tomatoes in oil, drained
4 red chilies, seeded and roughly chopped
extra-virgin olive oil, to loosen

2 large (around 4½ pounds) lamb shoulders

No getting around it, unless you are a masterly and proficient chopper, this is a job for a food processor. Cram everything for the herb paste in with a hefty twist of pepper and only a pinch of salt (the anchovies are salty). Pour in about a wine glass of olive oil—enough to get the blades moving, in other words—then press the pulse button, stopping to scrape everything down the sides a couple of times. You're aiming for a rusty-red "salsa verde" with a thick but nubbly texture. Scoop half the mixture into a bowl and stir in more olive oil to loosen. This will be your sauce, to serve with the lamb, so plastic wrap the top and chill it for up to 5 days, until needed. The rest will serve as a herb paste, to rub over the lamb shoulders. Of course, this can also be kept for a few days before using.

Rub the thick portion of the herb paste over the lamb shoulders, covering the entire surface. Preheat the oven to 425°F. Light the grill and wait until the coals are white hot and glowing in places. Quickly sear each lamb shoulder on the metal grate, until beginning to char on the outside, for no more than 10 minutes. You want to imbue the lamb with smoke, not cook it. Transfer both shoulders to a large roasting pan.

Roast in the preheated oven for 30 minutes. The lamb will be well-colored but shouldn't be burned. Immediately cover the pan in four layers of thick foil, sealing the edges tightly and trapping the heat in. Now wrap in a thick blanket or a few old towels. Set aside for 3 hours for rare; 4 hours for medium-rare. The shoulders will hold for an hour or so longer, if needed. Unwrap the lamb and slice each shoulder thickly on a board. Serve with the herb sauce.

GRILLED ARTICHOKES WITH ALMONDS

THOSE YOUNG, PURPLE ARTICHOKES ARE SUCH A TREAT but preparing them is, quite frankly, annoying. Large globe artichokes are far more amenable, proving greater square footage for the effort of trimming them and removing the choke. I stumbled upon this way of preparing them on the grill. The slightly blackened but tender artichokes work so well with a simple dressing and a handful of toasted almonds.

Start by whisking the garlic, balsamic vinegar, mustard, and olive oil together. This can be done a few days in advance and kept chilled.

Cut the top third from each artichoke, just enough so you can dig down with a teaspoon and pull out the hairy choke from the center. With a small paring knife, pare away the tough outside of the stalk and any tough leaves at the bottom. Stick a bay leaf into the center.

Make sure the grill coals are white hot, with no trace of flame. Wrap each artichoke tightly in foil and grill over indirect heat for 20 to 25 minutes. Once unwrapped, the artichokes should be tender and slightly charred at the edges.

Serve warm or cool, with a generous amount of dressing spooned over—concentrating on the centers—and the almonds and parsley scattered on top. The tops of the leaves will not be edible (the bases are) and need to be pulled away from the artichoke to eat, so provide a few fingerbowls with lemon slices.

ENOUGH FOR UP TO 10 WITH THE SALADS, IN PLACE OF THE LAMB
PREP 30 MINUTES
COOK 20 TO 25 MINUTES

FOR THE DRESSING
1 garlic clove, crushed
4 tablespoons balsamic vinegar
1 teaspoon whole grain mustard
¾ cup extra-virgin olive oil

FOR THE ARTICHOKES
10 globe artichokes
10 bay leaves
1 cup slivered almonds, toasted
handful of parsley, chopped

FOCACCIA BOARDS

When catering for large numbers, one occasionally has to compromise. Baking your own bread is obviously to be applauded. But what with smoking fish and cooking on a grill and all the other bits and pieces, something has to give. Get to know a local deli or baker stocking or producing good bread. Focaccia is lovely with this menu, but any rustic or crusty bread would do well. Get somebody to bring the bread for you on the morning of your event. I reckon to serve one large focaccia between four people using a menu such as this. Slice the bread no more than thirty minutes before it will be needed, covering with dish towels. Set up at least one "bread area" in the shade, with a wooden cutting board to pile the loaves on. Spoon butter into small dishes and stand butter knives in jam jars. You'll need extra-virgin olive oil for dipping, too. That way, you don't need to get involved in the business of serving it. A hand-painted sign is a nice touch; it need only say "bread" and can be as rustic as you like.

Having worked as a food stylist for many years, I have picked up a fair few ideas along the way. Here are some practical tips and styling touches intended only to inspire; hopefully they tread a line that is charming and attainable, without being prissy. Remember that good food and a happy party are the most important things, so don't get even remotely wound up about decoration schemes.

SEATING

It is important that everybody sits comfortably. That way, they will be relaxed and more inclined to enjoy the food. Simple cotton or linen seat pads can be made by covering foam pads or slim pillows with fabric. Even a very basic muslin or drape lining will look fabulous for very little cost. Sew ties at two corners, to tie the seat pad to the chair; pads will make any chair cooler and more comfortable.

Use whatever chairs you can find: plastic, wicker, padded, or wooden, always with the mindset that mismatching is a charming bonus. Even pillowed tree stumps look weirdly wonderful. If you are holding a wedding or similar celebration, swathes of slightly stiff fabric, tied around the chair backs in a bow, look very grand.

Sitting comfortably certainly doesn't have to involve chairs. Mezze night's Moroccan-ish menu (see page 175), for example, lends itself superbly to lounging on big pillows on a rug. The food could be set out on a low table in the middle, or simply laid out on the rug with everybody sitting around,

picnic-style. In desperate times, if the table is too small and you can't source enough chairs, you could sling a couple of planks (nothing splintery!) across the seats of at least three chairs so people can sit in between. You'll need a sturdy chair at each end and at least one to take the strain in the center. Leave no more than a generously seated bottom's length between each chair, for safety. Make it comfier with pillows and use magazines to even up any discrepancies in chair height, so everything is stable.

Try not to let things get so cramped that lifting a fork or an elbow is a battle; if space is that short, it would be far better to extend the tables slightly.

TABLES

Whether round or rectangular, if at all possible, it's best to keep the seating to one table, so go for "bolt-on" tables (ones that can be fitted together) where you can. Obviously, with numbers above a dozen, it's going to be tricky in most houses. In that case, keep the tables as close as you can without cramping anybody.

Trestle tables, constructed with a pair of saw-horses and a sturdy sheet of plywood, can be set up. Check the stability often in multiple places. If the table is on a lawn or soft ground, be prepared to put sheets of plywood down to form a temporary base. It will stop table legs, chairs, and high heels sinking into the grass.

Tablecloths in the same fabric or similar colors do a great job of bringing everything together and hiding any joins or formica that lie beneath.

BLOSSOM & BLOOM

Flowers on the table are the simplest, but most effective, decoration I know. Nothing should obscure anybody's view, nor take up too much space. Put just a few seasonal flowers into old jam jars, empty tea canisters, tin cans, or tin spice pots and set them on the table. In fall, use catkins or hardy herbs.

Separate children's tables are a fabulous idea. I remember delighting in the separate table my cousins and I shared at family gatherings. Leave the oldest child in charge, and keep an eye on proceedings.

DRINKS STATIONS

I like to keep drinks separate from the food, if at all possible, to keep queues and people-traffic to a minimum.

On a completely separate table, set up extra glasses or jam jars for cocktails and cordials. Have them lined up, complete with jaunty straws and ice in a chilled bowl. The cocktail ingredients —or cordials and soda —can be poured to taste. The table will look so pretty and it will simplify matters greatly.

LANTERNS & CANDLES

Fairy lights cover a multitude of sins after dark; string them up in trees, or over walls and canopies.

Lanterns, hung safely from branches or on sticks, make for a romantic evening setting. For an inexpensive alternative, try punching holes in empty tin cans, using thick gloves, a screwdriver, and a hammer, to make pretty tealight holders. Add string loops to the top to hang them by. Light the way to or from supper with bought paper lanterns, homemade tin can lanterns (as above), or glass lanterns, made by filling the bottoms of jam jars with sand and standing slim candles up in them. Citronella candles and torches will keep insects at bay on summer evenings. Those globular white or colored paper lanterns so beloved by students can be bought in varying sizes, ready to be strung and hung from trees. They will look beautiful in the daytime as well as at night and make the prettiest garlands. As, would you believe, do coffee filters. The unbleached or white filters can be bunched together and sewn through the center, or tied, to form a ruffled "flower." String these blossoms up on a length of twine or ribbon, to form a garland for very little cost. Coffee filters are also useful as liners for bowls of fruit, truffles, cakes, or brownies.

SEATING PLANS

I only bother with these when more than six guests are involved, or when trying to matchmake without being crashingly obvious. It does create a sense of formality, which isn't always a good thing, but you can have some fun in the planning and hopefully make sure conversation hums along energetically, if not nicely, on the day or night.

OTHER IDEAS

Slim wooden stakes, plunged into the ground, look ethereally lovely with fine strips of lightweight fabric tied to the tips. They will dance in the breeze.

Garden twine is invaluable for bunching, tying, stringing up lights, lanterns, and tealight jars and for grouping chopsticks, flatware, or napkins. Raffia or strips of muslin also do the job with the latter three.

Soften candles and jars by tying a scrap of cloth— something light and loose such as muslin is ideal —around the center and knotting it loosely.

If you're sitting outside and it's a chilly evening, offer blankets for those who feel the cold to drape over their laps.

Finishing Touches

Put your cynical tendencies aside and go with these ideas (unless we're talking about a party for the boys to watch the game and scarf down a pile of food). A few personal touches, which can be as simple as you like, really do create a sense of occasion.

The idea may seem a little gussied-up, but place settings are a sweet way to seat guests where you want them and pay homage to whatever season you find yourselves in. I am a great fan of using single fruits or vegetables, or simple objects. Tie an old-fashioned postal label—the pale gray sort with a punched hole and string ties—around the stalk or girth of said object, having first written names on them.

No time or wish to lay the table formally? Stick tied bundles of flatware into small buckets or pickle jars and spread them out on the table when you get a second, ready for guests to help themselves. Or, in each water tumbler, stick a napkin, a tied knife, fork, and spoon and a name tag. Perhaps a fresh blossom, too.

If you're hosting a large gathering and don't want to keep on shouting what everything is, make labels and/or write a menu. It needn't be a work of art, just your best writing on some nice card or paper is fine. Go to town if you like; an old typewriter makes delightful labels and menus. That way, everyone knows what's what and it is a fun touch.

SOME SUGGESTIONS:

SPRING AND SUMMER
Bunch of cherries
Sprig of lilac
Predinner cocktail in a jam jar, with a striped straw
Heirloom tomato
Paper fan
Globe artichoke
Bunch of fresh rosemary or thyme
A single shell
An old-fashioned English rose

FALL AND WINTER
Mini pumpkin
Small bunch of grapes
A perfect fig
A tiny, sealed jar of marmalade or citrus curd
Clementine or Sicilian lemon, with leaves
Cinnamon stick
Pine cone
Small pomegranate

SPLENDID STRAWBERRY AND VANILLA CAKE

**SERVES 50 TO 90 (SEE RECIPE
INTRODUCTION)**
PREP 3½ HOURS
COOK ABOUT 3½ HOURS

YOU WILL NEED:

3 deep, springform cake pans
 of 10½ inches, 9 inches, and
 8 inches

FOR THE BASE CAKE

generous 2⅓ cups superfine
 sugar
generous 2 cups (4 sticks)
 unsalted butter, very soft
8 eggs, at room temperature
4 cups self-rising flour
1½ teaspoons baking powder
½ teaspoon salt
generous ¾ cup ground almonds
scant ½ cup buttermilk
2½ teaspoons vanilla extract

FOR THE MIDDLE CAKE

1¾ cups superfine sugar
1½ cups (3 sticks) unsalted
 butter, very soft
6 eggs, at room temperature
scant 3 cups self-rising flour
½ teaspoon baking powder
generous pinch of salt
½ cup ground almonds
5 tablespoons buttermilk
1/2 teaspoons vanilla extract

FOR THE TOP CAKE

scant 1 cup superfine sugar
¾ cup (1½ sticks) unsalted
 butter, very soft
3 eggs, at room temperature
scant 1½ cups self-rising flour

NOW THIS IS A PROJECT.

We fruitcake haters have to stick to our guns. I would infinitely
prefer to eat this fresh, rather informal cake at a wedding or summer
celebration than any marzipan. Its vanilla sponge has to be sturdy
enough to hold up to being split and stacked, but, in spite of this, the
cake remains light to eat. The recipe is easily divided so, if you only
want to make one tier, just pick your size.

Black flecks of vanilla seed speckle the ivory frosting. To get the same
effect without vanilla beans, substitute 3 teaspoons of vanilla bean
paste, which can be found in grocery stores or online. Slicing wedding
cakes is a particular art. Work from the outside in, dividing the cake
by eye into a central circle and a surrounding ring. The surrounding
ring is cut into approximately 1¼- by 2-inch slices; the central circle
is divided into small wedges. Working on this principal makes a
rather scary total of ninety slices. Realistically, however, accounting
for less-than-expert cutting, it will give a slightly more reasonable
eighty servings. If you are more generous with your portions, plan on
the cake serving fifty to sixty. Leftovers freeze beautifully.

Preheat the oven to 350°F. Line the bottoms and sides of the three
pans with nonstick parchment paper, sticking it in place with butter.

The method is the same for each cake: with the paddle attachment
fitted on a food mixer, beat the sugar and butter until pale and light.
You can also do this with a wooden spoon and an energetic arm. Add
the eggs, one by one, as you continue to beat. If the mixture looks
curdled, add a spoonful of the flour and continue to beat. Sift the flour
and baking powder over and add the salt. With the speed on very low,
mix, stopping to scrape down the sides, until the dry ingredients are
just incorporated. Add the almonds, buttermilk, and vanilla, before
briefly mixing to form a firm batter. Scrape into the pan, flattening
out the batter with a spatula, then make a shallow dip in the center.
This accounts for the cake rising in the middle.

Bake in the center of the oven, leaving well alone for the first 45
minutes at least, lest the cake collapses when you open the door.
Bake the largest cake for about 1½ hours, the middle cake for about
1 hour 10 minutes, and the small cake for about 55 minutes. They
should be golden and well risen. When a skewer is inserted, it should
come out clean. Let the cakes rest in their pans for a few minutes,
then turn out onto wire racks and let cool completely.

CONTINUED . . .

¼ teaspoon baking powder
pinch of salt
¼ cup ground almonds
scant 3 tablespoons buttermilk
¾ teaspoon vanilla extract

FOR THE FROSTING
scant 2¼ cups unsalted butter,
    very soft
2¼ pounds cream cheese, at
    room temperature
2 vanilla beans, split and seeds
    scraped out, or 3 teaspoons
    vanilla paste or extract
scant 8 cups confectioners'
    sugar, sifted, or to taste

**FOR THE FILLING AND
    TOPPING**
1¾ cups good-quality strawberry
    jam
5½ cups strawberries, hulled
    and sliced

It is highly likely you won't want to fill or frost the cakes immediately. They will keep, well wrapped, for a couple of days. Any more than that and I would advise you to freeze them. Beg or borrow freezer space from a cake-hating neighbor if you don't have enough yourself. Wrap in several layers of plastic wrap and freeze for up to 3 months. Defrost slowly overnight when needed.

The cream cheese frosting can be made up to 5 days ahead and kept in a sealed container (or several containers, considering the amount) in the refrigerator. The most important point is that the butter must be very soft and the cream cheese must be at room temperature. If one or both are too cold, they will not whip to a smooth frosting and you may get tiny pebbles of hard butter suspended throughout.

With the paddle attachment in place, beat the butter and cream cheese together in an electric mixer. Keep beating for about 4 minutes, stopping to scrape down the sides of a bowl with a spatula. Add the vanilla seeds, paste, or extract with the mixer running.

Turn the speed down very low and slowly add the confectioners' sugar. If you add it too quickly, a sugar cloud will surround you. Keep adding until all the sugar is incorporated, and then taste for sweetness. If you prefer a more sugary frosting, add scant 1–2⅔ cups more, remembering that the cake and jam filling are already sweet. The more sugar you add, the thicker the frosting will become. Increase the speed for the last few seconds, to give the frosting a last whip. Use immediately or cover and chill for later use. (Chilled frosting is easier to work with.)

Carefully split the cakes in half with a serrated knife, taking off any risen "domes" at the same time, if necessary. Have the jam and strawberries at hand. The cakes will sit upside down to make them easier to ice and neater to present, meaning the top half of each will now become the base and vice versa.

Spread the lower half of the largest cake with a ¾-inch or so layer of cream cheese frosting, leaving a small border at the edge to allow for the frosting oozing out when the top half is applied. Cover with a tightly wedged layer of sliced strawberries, again, being mindful that they won't bulge out of the sides later. Spread the top half with jam, again leaving a small border at the edge. Place this on top of the base cake and press gently to seal. Run a layer of frosting around the outside of the middle join, to seal in the jam and strawberries and prevent any pink bleeding out.

Repeat with the remaining two cakes.

A tiered design such as this needs support to prevent the cake from collapsing, which is where the doweling comes in. Measure one rod against the largest cake and mark the height of the cake. Cut into three or four equal lengths with a saw knife. Do the same with the next doweling rod and the middle cake. Stick three or four vertical rods into each of the larger cakes. They should be evenly spaced and hidden within the cake. If they stick up at all, trim them down.

Using a palette knife, spread a very thin layer of frosting over the sides of all three cakes, making it slightly thicker when you spread it over the tops. It doesn't have to be neat. This is called the crumb layer and traps any crumbs that could disrupt the finish of the frosted cake. If the entire cake is to be served from a large wooden board, you will need no cake board beneath. If you intend to present it on a cake stand, first sit the base tier on the cake board. I must confess, I don't always do this and I haven't been bitten yet . . .

Once the largest cake is sitting on its chosen base, cut or tear four wide strips of parchment paper. Tuck the long sides of all these strips just underneath the cake, to form a wide border all the way around the base, to protect the surface below as you spread the frosting on.

Sit the middle cake on top, off-center, so that one vertical edge lines up with a vertical edge of the large cake. Do the same with the top tier, lining the "back" of the entire cake up carefully; it should be completely vertical with no similarities to a certain tower from Pisa. The finished arrangement will be like three steps. Stick the remaining wooden dowel vertically through the three cakes, from top to bottom. Trim any excess so that it is completely hidden.

Dollop frosting onto the top of the top cake. Working in confident, sweeping motions, work the frosting over and across the top to the edges. Now work the overspill around the sides, keeping the knife almost vertical to create a clean finish. Keep adding more frosting as needed, sweeping it across and down until the entire three cakes are covered thickly and evenly. You will need to spend quite a bit of time walking around the cake and viewing it from every angle to check that no sponge is showing. Keep the cake cool: sun and heat are the sworn enemies of cream cheese frosting, though curious pets come a close second. The frosted cake will sit in the cool for a few hours without harm. Even overnight is not out of the question, in a cold pantry. Just before serving, decorate the cake sparingly with fresh, unsprayed flowers, wild strawberries, and wild strawberry leaves. Less is more.

YOU WILL NEED:

3 x 12-inch wooden or plastic
   doweling rods, ready to cut
   to size

saw knife

thin 12-inch diameter cake board
   (optional)

parchment paper, to assist with
   frosting the cake

fresh, unsprayed roses, sweet
   pea flowers, wild strawberries,
   and strawberry leaves, to
   decorate

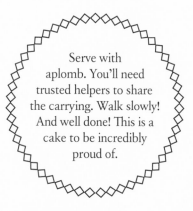

Serve with aplomb. You'll need trusted helpers to share the carrying. Walk slowly! And well done! This is a cake to be incredibly proud of.

DRINKS STATION: BASIL LIMEADE, RASPBERRY CRUSH, AND ELDERFLOWER VODKA

ADORN A SEPARATE TABLE WITH ICE BOWLS, soda, extra glasses, stirrers, and muddlers. Set labeled pitchers of these drinks out and direct your guests to the table with a sign and an arrow. It's a good idea to have somebody man the station, ready to top off the levels, and to keep the elderflower vodka away from the kids.

ENOUGH FOR 20 TALL (DILUTED) GLASSES, EASILY HALVED
PREP 20 MINUTES, PLUS COOLING

3¾ cups granulated sugar
2 large handfuls of Greek basil or chopped standard basil leaves
juice of 24 limes
still or sparking water, to top off
4 limes, sliced, to serve
ice cubes, to serve

BASIL LIMEADE

I have used Greek basil to make this fresh limeade with excellent results, though regular chopped basil is perfectly fine. This recipe also works well with mint.

Put the sugar in a large pan with 4 cups of water and 1 large handful of basil. Bring to a boil slowly, stirring to dissolve the sugar. Once no grains of sugar remain, turn off the heat. Set aside to cool, then strain through a fine strainer. Combine the sugar syrup with the lime juice and dilute with still or sparkling water to taste. Serve in pitchers with the lime slices, the remaining basil leaves, and ice if you like.

ENOUGH FOR 20
PREP 15 MINUTES

scant 5 cups ripe raspberries
juice of 8 lemons
¾ cup superfine sugar
chilled lemonade or sparkling water, to top off
Chambord (optional)

RASPBERRY CRUSH

This is a great one for kids (without the Chambord). If the seeds of the rustic crushed raspberries bother you, strain them out before diluting.

In a large mixing bowl, crush the raspberries, lemon juice, and sugar with a potato masher. Let macerate for 10 minutes, then divide between two pitchers and top off with lemonade or sparkling water (depending on how sweet you like your drinks). Adults could add a little Chambord, that delightfully tacky raspberry liqueur.

ENOUGH FOR 20
PREP 10 MINUTES

2 cups elderflower cordial
4 cups good-quality vodka
juice of 15 limes
ice cubes, to serve

ELDERFLOWER VODKA

A cheeky little cocktail number that you can serve straight, over ice, or top off with soda water in tall, ice-filled glasses.

Combine the cordial, vodka, and lime juice. Chill until needed. Serve over ice, as it is, or diluted with sparkling water.

FESTIVAL GLAMPING

A HEARTY VEGETABLE SOUP | **SMOKY PEA AND HAM SOUP** | *Pressed steak or antipasti sandwiches* | **RED ONION RELISH WITH PORT** | DEEP AND CHEWY FLAPJACKS | LEMON AND CARDAMOM CHICKEN THIGHS | GEORGINA'S TOASTED COUSCOUS WITH GREEN LEAVES

There is a world of difference between glamping—glamorous camping to you and me—and proper, hardy camping. In turn, there is a great deal of difference between glamping in the great outdoors and boutique camping, at music festivals. I wouldn't be so foolish as to suggest you trek over hill and valley with a two-man tent on your back and whip up a vegetable soup for your supper. More likely a can of tepid baked beans in that situation. But at least my flapjacks (page 92) will provide trekking fuel, so all is not lost.

Glamping is camping with a few creature comforts; with comfy beds and cool boxes, or mini refrigerators plugged into an electric hook up; with camper vans or in a spacious bell tent. Camping for softies and not the real, rugged deal, in other words.

These recipes are mostly intended to be made before you leave, so you have some good food to get you started. A couple, namely the pressed sandwiches and sticky chicken with couscous and greens, depend on some sort of cooler to keep them chilled for a few hours. Unless transported in a Thermos, the soups will need to be reheated over a camping stove.

As for music festivals, I know how this one goes. Before you know it, you'll be drinking lemonade for breakfast and eating chocolate for lunch and, by supper time, you'll either be in front of a stage, or you'll be enticed over to the plethora of gourmet burger and snack stalls that most large festivals boast. The trouble being that the festival tickets, travel, and paraphernalia cost at least a week's wages, so you might not have fistfuls of money to burn. At least you can take a good soup along, or a sandwich, or a batch of flapjacks. Something homemade and wholesome to keep you ticking along for a day at least. Just wait until day three, when cold beans from a can will seem practically gourmet . . .

FOOD

1 A good amount of **drinking water**.
2 Flapjacks (*see page 92*) or similarly dense cereal bars, cakes, and cookies.
3 A fabulous **sandwich**, kept cool with a freezer block, for the first day only. One that won't mind getting squashed (*see page 91*).

4 Apples, dried fruit, and nuts as a slightly healthier source of energy. Don't take bananas; they will get squashed.
5 Baked beans.
6 Bread. Something that will keep for a day or two, such as sourdough.

7 Cooking oil in a small bottle.
8 Marshmallows.
9 Salt, pepper, ketchup.

COOKING & Food Kit

1 A light **cooler** with frozen freezer blocks for milk, juice, cheese, bacon, and so on.
2 Matches or a lighter.
3 a) **Fire lighters** to encourage damp wood to burn; b) or a **camping stove** with gas.

4 Camping pans or light cooking pans.
5 An **oven mitt** or thick cloth.
6 Washing-up liquid and a scourer.
7 Long tongs and a **wooden spoon**.

8 Camping plates/bowls, basic flatware, mugs, or cups.
9 A **pocket knife**. Opinels are beautiful.
10 A **vegetable peeler**.

. . . AND DON'T LEAVE HOME WITHOUT

1 Sunscreen.
2 A flashlight.
3 Trash bags for garbage.
4 Anti-bacterial hand wipes.

A HEARTY VEGETABLE SOUP

INSTEAD OF BARLEY, YOU COULD USE QUINOA; it won't need any precooking so can be added to the olive oil with the vegetables. A grain of some sort adds extra nourishment that will be especially welcome when an energy boost is needed. This soup needs no accompaniment.

Extras freeze perfectly for a few months. Although the vegetables need to be finely diced to make them easy to eat, I don't bother to skin the tomatoes and I see no need to remove their seeds. This is a hearty soup, not a dinner party soup (I don't think I'd want one of those anyway). If you want to use a can of plum tomatoes instead of fresh, smush them down a little and add halfway through the simmering time to cook out any "tinny" taste.

The soup will keep, chilled, for a good five days. Reheat until piping hot, but you can allow it to cool and eat at room temperature if it's a very hot day. This is actually a nicer idea than it may sound!

Cover the barley with plenty of water in a pan, add a pinch of salt, and bring to a boil. Cover and simmer gently for 15 minutes, then drain and set aside.

Heat the olive oil in a large pan and add all the vegetables except the spinach, fava beans, and tomatoes. Season with a little salt to draw the water out and gently cook, stirring often, for 10 minutes, until softened but not colored.

Add the stock and parcooked barley, and bring to a boil. Reduce the heat to the point where the soup is simmering nicely. Let simmer for 30 minutes, then add the spinach, fava beans, and tomatoes and continue to simmer for another 5 to 10 minutes. Remove from the heat and stir in the basil. Taste and adjust the seasoning as needed, then serve or ladle into large Thermos containers, or cool and chill, ready to reheat later.

I very much doubt this would be the case at a festival, but if you make this at home and have any good extra-virgin olive oil on hand, or even better, fresh pesto, add a little to each serving before eating.

SERVES 8
PREP 20 MINUTES
COOK ABOUT 1 HOUR

scant 1 cup pearl barley or spelt

3 tablespoons olive oil

1 large fennel bulb, trimmed and finely chopped

12 smallish, young carrots, scrubbed and finely diced

12 new potatoes, scrubbed and finely diced

6 zucchini, trimmed and finely diced

bunch of scallions, trimmed and finely sliced

4 cups good vegetable stock

1¼ pounds spinach leaves, washed and drained

7 ounces fresh or frozen young fava beans (shelled weight)

6 plum tomatoes, diced

handful of basil leaves, shredded (optional)

SMOKY PEA AND HAM SOUP

**SERVES 8 GENEROUSLY,
   MORE IF YOU SERVE
   IN MUGS**
PREP 15 MINUTES, PLUS 1 TO 4
   HOURS SOAKING
COOK 1¼ HOURS

1 smoked ham hock
1 large onion, roughly chopped
1 large carrot, roughly chopped
2 celery stalks, roughly chopped
bouquet garni of 2 bay leaves,
   2 sprigs of thyme, and 2 sprigs
   of rosemary
scant 2⅔ cups green or yellow
   split peas
3½ cups fresh or frozen green
   peas, shelled weight

EVEN SUMMER NIGHTS CAN GET CHILLY—especially
when the inevitable drizzle gets the better of the sun—but a mug
of soup, made a day or two in advance and heated up when needed,
will ward off the damp. This is an essential at English summer
parties, made brighter and lighter with a good helping of fresh or
frozen peas.

A ham hock can be ridiculously salty, so be sure to soak it in plenty
of cold water before cooking. At least one to four hours of soaking,
with a couple of water changes, will prevent any excess salt from
spoiling your soup.

Soak the ham hock as mentioned in the recipe introduction. When
ready to make the soup, put everything apart from the fresh or
frozen green peas in a large, lidded pan with 2 quarts of
water and bring to a boil. Reduce the heat to low and let putter-
putter gently, lid on, for 1½ hours. Add the fresh or frozen peas
and cook for another 5 minutes. Turn the heat off and remove the
bouquet garni, then carefully fish out the ham hock, dropping it into
a bowl.

Let the hock cool a little before shredding or chopping the meat
quite finely, removing and discarding the skin, fat, and bone as you
go. Set aside.

Puree the soup in the pan with a stick blender, or pour into an
upright blender in two batches. I don't puree this thoroughly, so the
soup retains some texture, but blend until smooth if you prefer.

Return the soup to the heat, along with all but 3 tablespoons of the
shredded ham, if you will be garnishing the soup; otherwise just add
it all now. Taste and add more salt if needed, it will certainly need a
little black pepper. Dilute with water if the soup seems too thick to
you; the consistency is supposed to be hearty though, not thin.

Serve hot, scattered with the reserved ham if the circumstances
warrant garnish and fripperies. The soup will keep chilled for up to 5
days; reheat until piping hot before eating.

PRESSED STEAK OR ANTIPASTI SANDWICHES

INSTEAD OF FILLING INDIVIDUAL LOAVES or sandwiches, you can hollow out one large loaf, fill it with the ingredients, and press for a few hours before slicing and eating.

If you are using small loaves of bread, cut them in half and pull out most of the doughy crumb with your fingers, leaving a study shell. The middles make excellent bread crumbs, so freeze them for another day.

Place a griddle or skillet over high heat until smoking hot. Rub the steaks with a little olive oil and the rosemary. Season generously. Sear the steaks in the hot pan, literally for just a minute each side, until browned but still medium rare. Remove to a plate and let cool. Slice each steak into four and reserve the juices.

Drizzle the insides of the loaves, or one side of each bread slice, with olive oil. Layer four loaf bases or bread slices (oiled side up), a spoonful of steak juices (not too much or it will get soggy), 1 tablespoon red onion relish, six pieces of steak, and some arugula. Layer the other four with the antipasti vegetables, mozzarella, and basil leaves.

Replace all the loaf tops or top with a second slice of bread (oiled side down), and wrap each firmly in plastic wrap. Place a weight (such as a can of beans) on top of each and let press in the refrigerator for 2 to 5 hours before unwrapping and eating.

MAKES 8 ROLLS OR SANDWICHES
PREP 20 MINUTES, PLUS 2 TO 5 HOURS PRESSING
COOK 2 MINUTES

8 small, rustic loaves of bread, or 16 thin slices of rustic bread
extra-virgin olive oil

FOR THE STEAK
6 minute steaks
1 teaspoon minced rosemary
4 tablespoons Red Onion Relish with Port (see below)
handful of wild arugula leaves

FOR THE ANTIPASTI
11 ounces antipasti (char-grilled peppers, artichokes, eggplants, or tomatoes in oil, drained weight)
2 balls buffalo mozzarella, drained thoroughly and sliced
handful of basil leaves

RED ONION RELISH WITH PORT

A NATTY LITTLE NUMBER to have in your repertoire. You can add this to stews, gravies, and meat sauces for a touch of sweetness.

Add the onions to a very large pan with the oil and salt. Cook over low heat for a couple of minutes, then cover tightly and cook for 40 minutes, stirring occasionally. Remove the lid and add the port, increasing the heat slightly. Let the liquid bubble away, stirring to stop it catching, then tip in the sugar and stir until the onions begin to turn golden. This will take longer than you think! Finish with the vinegar and thyme, again, cooking until the liquid has gone.

Pour into sterilized jars—sealing them tightly—and keep in the refrigerator. Aim to use within a month or so.

MAKES 2 LARGE JAM JARS
PREP 20 MINUTES
COOK ABOUT 1 HOUR PLUS 40 MINUTES

4½ pounds red onions, halved and finely sliced
2 tablespoons olive oil
large pinch of salt
generous 1 cup port
½ cup superfine sugar
4 tablespoons balsamic vinegar
2 tablespoons thyme leaves

DEEP AND CHEWY FLAPJACKS

BEST NOT TO KID YOURSELF ABOUT THE FACTS HERE: this ain't no diet food. Flapjacks are no more than oats suspended in butter toffee—last time I looked, that combination wasn't high on the list of recommended health foods. But they are incredibly good. These enormous ones are perfect for sharing and will fuel a great deal of rainy festival-traipsing. Reasons enough to make them, without the pseudo "cereal bar" label, I hope.

Do replace some of the oats with seeds, nuts, or dried fruit if you would like to add more interest to this delightfully plain version.

Preheat the oven to 300°F. Use a convection rather than a fan oven, if possible.

In your largest pan, melt the butter, sugar, and syrup together over low heat, stirring until no grains of sugar remain. Keep cooking and stirring until the toffee is bubbling and smooth. Stir in all the oats and continue to stir over the heat for 5 minutes. You want them to soften in the toffee. Mix in the salt and turn off the heat.

Press firmly into a 12 by 8-inch pan, lined with nonstick parchment paper that reaches up the sides. Bake for 1 hour 10 minutes, or until deeply golden at the edges but still a tiny bit wobbly right in the center.

Dip a wooden spoon in cold water (to stop it sticking) and use the back to press the flapjack down again firmly. Set aside to cool in the pan; it's very important that you don't disturb, score, or cut the flapjacks now or they won't hold together. Let them get completely cool. That means overnight for best results, or a minimum of 4 hours if you're really in a pickle.

Tip the whole flapjack out onto a board, remove the paper, and cut into as many pieces as you desire. They'll last in an airtight tin, in a cool place, for up to a week.

**MAKES 12 RIDICULOUSLY
LARGE FLAPJACKS, OR
16 SLIGHTLY MORE
REASONABLE ONES**
PREP 10 MINUTES
COOK 1 HOUR 10 MINUTES

scant 3 cups butter
1³/₄ cups brown sugar
1 cup dark corn syrup
4³/₄ cups jumbo rolled oats
3¹/₂ cups rolled oats or oatmeal
   (I use half spelt)
pinch of salt

LEMON AND CARDAMOM CHICKEN THIGHS

SERVES 4 HUNGRY PEOPLE
PREP 15 MINUTES, PLUS
   MARINATING
COOK 45 MINUTES

4 tablespoons extra-virgin
   olive oil
4 tablespoons thin honey
2 garlic cloves, crushed
finely grated zest of 2 unwaxed
   lemons and juice of 1
6 green cardamom pods, crushed
   so they split
1 teaspoon coarsely ground
   black pepper
8 large chicken thighs (or legs),
   with bone and skin
1 tablespoon sesame seeds

MAKE PEACE WITH YOURSELF WHEN EATING THE
CHICKEN COLD AT A PICNIC as the skin will have lost much
of its crunch. I still think it's delicious, in the way that brined and
ready-cooked chicken is. If you are making these to eat hot, the skin
will be crisp and generally most appealing.

Incidentally, it's quite possible to make this on a camping stove,
keeping the heat low to cook the chicken right through. But, in
the absence of camping paraphernalia, I'd recommend cooking
the thighs in advance. Chill them down thoroughly and transport
chicken, couscous, and greens (see right) in airtight containers,
tucked into a padded cooler, and buffered by a couple of small ice
blocks. It should keep you away from those expensive burger vans
for a few more hours at least.

Marinate the chicken. In a nonmetallic, ovenproof dish, combine all
the ingredients except the sesame seeds with a large pinch of salt.
Cover and chill for at least 8 hours, or up to 2 days.

Preheat the oven to 425°F. Turn the chicken pieces skin-side
up, baste well, and slide into the oven. Immediately reduce the
temperature to 375°F and roast the chicken for about 35 minutes,
basting with the juices now and then, until deeply golden;
10 minutes before the end of cooking, sprinkle the sesame
seeds over the skin.

Serve warm if you're planning to eat at home, otherwise skim off
any visible fat by tilting the pan, then keep basting with the juices
as the chicken cools. Chill thoroughly and eat within 48 hours, with
Georgina's Toasted Couscous with Green Leaves (see right).

GEORGINA'S TOASTED COUSCOUS WITH GREEN LEAVES

MY DEAR FRIEND GEORGINA AND I MET AT COOKING SCHOOL and have been partners in crime ever since. Among other things, Georgina champions a winning way with Israeli (giant) or standard couscous that may be adapted to most grains and grain-like ingredients, think quinoa, millet, spelt, barley—the list goes on. Before simmering, you toast them in a skillet with a little oil and/ or butter, stirring often. Once golden and fragrant, the nuttiness of each grain will be amplified, lending an added resonance.

Unless you are a vegetarian and are making this separately, pack the chicken in the same box as the couscous, so the chicken juices add to and sweeten the dressing. Transport the leaves separately, or lay on top of the chicken and couscous, only mixing in when you eat, to keep them sprightly.

Heat 1 tablespoon of the oil in a large skillet and add the couscous. Toast over medium-high heat, stirring often, until it turns a deep golden brown and smells toasted.

Cover the couscous with water—you'll need about 3 cups—add a pinch of salt and bring to a boil. Simmer, stirring often, for about 14 minutes, until all the water has been absorbed. Remove from the heat and let cool.

Stir in the remaining oil, the lemon zest and juice, herbs, and scallions. Season to taste and eat with the cardamom chicken thighs and a pile of the green leaves, folding them into the chicken juices and the couscous to dress as you eat.

SERVES 4
PREP 15 MINUTES
COOK ABOUT 15 MINUTES

3 tablespoons olive oil
generous 1 cup Israeli (giant) or
    standard couscous
finely grated zest of 1 unwaxed
    lemon and a squeeze of juice
large handful each of mint and
    parsley leaves, minced
4 scallions, very finely chopped
2 handfuls of mixed leaves, such
    as arugula, watercress, young
    sorrel, or baby spinach

BEACH CRICKET BARBECUE FOR 6

BROWN BUTTER DABS | **A PICNIC POTATO SALAD** | *Pickled red onion and cucumber salad* | **BLUEBERRY, ALMOND, AND VANILLA CHOUX BUNS**

Frying local fish on a fire; playing ragtag ball games; sipping an honest and unfussy cocktail as the light fades—the most memorable summer days are made of these.

Setting up a base camp, however, with just a few rustic luxuries, adds to the occasion greatly. The extent of your beach barbecue paraphernalia will depend very much upon location; basket of food and drink aside, a sturdy skillet, matches, and a rug to sit on are all that's needed for the most basic beach supper. Perhaps a cricket bat and ball, too, or bocce or Frisbee if cricket is a puzzle to you. Firewood—and even fish—the beach and sea can provide.

First off, finding out if it's legal to build a fire on the beach you've chosen is pretty vital. Of course, there are usually signs about that will let you know, in no uncertain terms. If you're lucky enough to be able to build a fire, as always, leave everything as you found it. That means dousing fires with water or wet sand and taking garbage away with you.

When it comes to the menu, most of it can be prepared in advance. The fish will need sizzling and the choux buns are best filled on site, but that's about it. Both the salads won't mind being made that morning, along with the vanilla cream for the buns.

Nostalgic soft drinks are a must. Tuck them into a bucket of ice. I also have a weakness for simple cocktails shaken in glass jars. Pop your chosen ingredients, say, for a gin and tonic—a wedge of fresh lime (squeezed in), ice, and gin—in a jam jar, screw on the lid, and shake vigorously. Top off with as much tonic as you want and plunge a straw in.

Beach cricket, tidal pooling, sunbathing, paddling, and swimming should keep everybody happily occupied and, with any luck, there'll still be a few cubes of ice left for that drink once the sun goes down.

BROWN BUTTER DABS

SERVES 6
PREP VERY LITTLE
COOK AROUND 6 MINUTES PER
  PAIR OF DABS

about 6 very fresh dabs
  assuming 1 per person, more if
  the fish are smaller than about
  14 ounces each
3 small cans (about 2½ ounces
  each) of brown shrimps
lemons, a squeeze of juice and
  wedges to serve
a little chopped parsley (optional)

MY FAMILY IS LUCKY ENOUGH TO OWN A LITTLE HIDEAWAY BY THE SEA. The beach is a quiet beauty; perfect for those impromptu cricket and Frisbee games, and poking around tidal pools, once the tide sweeps out. Fittingly, we shot the accompanying photographs there.

Nearby Rye, on the south coast of England, houses a fleet of fishing boats, and the fish for sale is some of the best and freshest I've seen. The underused dab, a native flatfish similar to flounder, I suppose, but much smaller, is impressively good value and delicious. Give me a delicate dab or two rather than a slab of imported tuna any day.

Canned shrimp, already beautifully spiced and set in clarified butter, are a great boon for the outdoor cook here. If you forget the parsley, and I frequently do, all you need take to the beach are the shrimp, dabs, lemons, and seasoning.

Make a neat slit on the white belly side of the dabs—you're looking for the soft spot just below the head—and remove the entrails. This shouldn't be a messy job. Rinse well.

You'll need a heavy-bottomed pan to cook the fish, preferably one that will hold a couple of dabs at a time. Balance the pan safely over a hot flame, assuming the heat source is a campfire, and add the butter from the top of a shrimp pot. It should sizzle briskly.

Add two fish, brown-sides down, and fry until golden and crisp. Add all the canned shrimps from the can and their remaining butter and turn the fish over. Again, cook until the fish is turning golden. Remove from the heat, shower with lemon juice, salt, and pepper and, should you have it, a little chopped parsley. Serve right away and get on with cooking the remaining fish in the same way.

BASIC RULES & GUIDELINES
of beach cricket

CRICKET LOVERS are a passionate bunch. I know it isn't commonly played in the United States, but the rules are easy to understand, especially if you're familiar with baseball, and this incarnation of the game is a hoot. Usually, cricket is played on a manicured grass field in opposing teams of twelve; this is a very relaxed and informal version, destined for beaches and fileds on sunny days. You'll find most of the rules are far from traditional . . .

You'll need quite a bit of space for starters;
this isn't a game for crowded beaches. Mark out a line in the sand for the bowler (the pitcher) to start from and the batsman (or batter) to run to. This is the start of the wicket or cricket pitch, which can be anything from 30 to 60 feet in length. The other essentials are a bat, a ball, and sticks of some sort to form the stumps or wicket (two or three vertical sticks at about thigh-height with a little stick balanced horizontally on top. Driftwood is a good source). The wicket should be at the opposite end of the pitch to the bowler—it is what the bowler aims at. Improvise as needed; we use a tennis ball on the beach, and a baseball bat will do fine in lieu of a cricket bat.

EVERYBODY IS IN PLAY AT ALL TIMES.
There is no sitting on the sidelines waiting to bat in beach cricket. Divide into two even teams if you must, but every player, no matter which side they are on or how big the teams, has to put maximum effort into fielding.

EACH "OVER" USUALLY CONSISTS OF SIX BALLS
(think of it as a set of successive pitches), bowled at the wicket by the bowler. The batsman stands in front of the wicket and tries to hit each ball as far as he can, or in a way that will enable him to run to the marked bowling line from the wicket—and back—before the ball is returned to the bowler or thrown at the wicket. Each length of the pitch is a "run" and the tip of the bat must be tapped on the ground at the end for a run to qualify. When returning to the wicket, the batsman must shout "IN!" The aim for the batsman, and the batting team, is to get as many runs as possible.

The aim for the fielding team
—or fielders—is to get the batsman "OUT." The fielders spread out around the cricket pitch and attempt to catch the batted ball and throw it back to hit the wicket while the batsman is running. If you've played baseball, you'll get the idea. Just think of the wicket as a single base to aim at.

MAIN WAYS TO GET THE BATSMAN OUT:
Catch the batted ball before it has hit the ground, as you would in baseball; throw the ball at the wicket and dislodge the little stick on top while the batsman is away from it, as mentioned above; bowl to directly hit the wicket, dislodging the little stick on top.

IT IS UP TO THE PLAYERS TO DECIDE HOW MANY "OVERS" THE GAME WILL BE ON THE DAY.
If no one can be bothered to keep count, the bowler has a right to bowl two more balls from the time somebody questions whether the over has been played or not. This is beach cricket after all . . .

HAVE A GOOD SUPPLY OF TENNIS BALLS AT THE READY. You're bound to lose the odd one to a watery grave.

Parents and grandparents are not allowed to umpire
unless they swear to be utterly fair and non-biased for or against offspring. If no agreement can be reached on a decision, a compromise can be found, the "last man standing" rule applies: first team to leave the playing area forfeits the wicket. That includes hitting into the water.

A BATSMAN CANNOT BOWL STRAIGHT AWAY IF HE HAS JUST BEEN "GIVEN OUT."

DOGS DO COUNT AS FIELDERS,
but only if they return the ball on command. Running off with it does not count. The dog is on the same side as his or her owner, or nearest relative of the owner. If a ball **hits** a dog, however, the batsman is immediately out and must apologize profusely.

TO QUALIFY AS A NO BALL, the ball has to hit the ground a good person's length in front of the batsman.

To qualify as a wide,
the ball has to be thrown further to one side than the batsman can reach at full extension.

UNLESS THEY ARE PARTICULARLY GOOD AT CRICKET,
it is usual to give children first ball's grace, at least until they get their eye in.

IF A BATSMAN MISSES
three consecutive (good) balls, he is declared out.

If nobody can be be bothered to keep score at all,
the winner is the player deemed to have shown the most sporting prowess. Assuming this sporting prowess runs to swimming and/or paddling, the winner should always be thrown in the sea by the other players.

A PICNIC POTATO SALAD

I FAVOR WAXY POTATOES, SUCH AS ROUND RED HERE, AS THE POTATO OF CHOICE; it soaks up a dressing quite beautifully when warm. The trick, and there is only one—this is just a (very good) potato salad after all—is to get everything chopped and prepped while the potatoes simmer away. As soon as the spuds are drained, douse them in the dressing. There will be a generous amount, allowing for a fair bit to soak in. Serve just-warm or cool.

Simmer the potatoes in salted boiling water for 18 to 20 minutes, or until tender, as this will depend greatly on size. While they are cooking, whisk the oil, vinegar, mustard, and sugar together. Season generously with salt and pepper. Taste and adjust as you like; the dressing should be feisty.

Drain the potatoes well, tip into a bowl, and add the dressing. Mix well, then fold in the scallions and herbs, reserving the cress. Leave until warm or completely cool, turning the potatoes over occasionally. Tumble the mustard cress through just before serving.

SERVES 6
PREP 15 MINUTES
COOK ABOUT 20 MINUTES, PLUS COOLING

2¼ pounds new potatoes, a waxy variety that actually tastes of something, halved if large
5 tablespoons extra-virgin olive oil
3 tablespoons good red wine vinegar, or any quality vinegar you fancy
1 tablespoon whole grain mustard
pinch of superfine sugar
1 bunch of scallions, trimmed and sliced
small bunch of chives, snipped
handful of tarragon leaves, chopped
handful of snipped mustard cress

PICKLED RED ONION AND CUCUMBER SALAD

QUICK PICKLING FOR BEGINNERS. Granted, this becomes more of a piquant salad, but the onion makes a mild introduction to the addictive world of pickles.

Warm the sugar, salt, and vinegar with a splash of water over very low heat, stirring until just dissolved. Let cool, then add the onion, mix well, and set aside for at least 15 minutes or up to 1 hour. More if you like. The onions will mellow and lighten in color prettily, turning their pickling liquid to a blushing pink.

Add the remaining ingredients and a grind of pepper; it shouldn't need any salt, but taste and adjust as you like.

SERVES 6
PREP 20 MINUTES, PLUS STEEPING

2½ tablespoons superfine sugar
large pinch of salt
5 tablespoons red wine vinegar
2 small red onions, halved and very finely sliced
½ large cucumber, peeled, halved, seeded, and sliced
a few radishes, trimmed, scrubbed, and finely sliced
small handful of mint leaves, torn
a handful of radish sprouts

BLUEBERRY, ALMOND, AND VANILLA CHOUX BUNS

I ORIGINALLY WANTED TO FINISH THIS MENU WITH A BIG PARIS BREST—one of those enormous choux pastry rings, scattered with almonds and fit to burst with pastry cream and nontraditional blueberries—but the logistics of transporting it to the beach, let alone eating it, inspired a rethink. Manageable little buns encrusted with golden almonds can be filled just about anywhere and are easy to carry when still unfilled.

Once cooked and cooled, the buns can be frozen if it makes life easier. Open-freeze, spaced out on trays, then, once hard, transfer to freezer bags, seal well, and keep for up to two months. Defrost and recrisp in a low oven before halving and filling as below.

This is the way I was taught to make choux pastry at cooking school. Fold a large piece of paper (wax will do) in half and open back out again. The fold will be your flour chute. Sift the flour a couple of times, add the salt, and pour onto the paper.

Preheat the oven to 375°F. Put the butter and ¾ cup water in a pan and set over low-ish heat to melt the butter. As soon as the butter has melted, increase the heat to high so the liquid reaches a fierce boil as quickly as possible.

Immediately tip the flour down its paper chute into the boiling liquid. Remove from the heat and beat vigorously with a wooden spoon. As soon as the mixture looks smooth and comes away from the sides of the pan, stop beating. Otherwise it will become greasy. Spread out onto a plate to cool quickly. When cool enough to touch comfortably, transfer to a mixing bowl and, using a handheld whisk, beat in the egg, a little at a time. You may not need it all, so only keep adding until a scoop of the choux drops reluctantly from its spoon when jerked sharply.

Fit a pastry bag with a large, plain tip and fill with the choux. To make this easier with only two hands, balance the open pastry bag in a large glass, folding the excess fabric over the top as you spoon the pastry in.

Line one large, or two smaller, baking sheets with nonstick parchment paper and scatter with half the slivered almonds.

MAKES ABOUT 20
PREP 20 TO 30 MINUTES
COOK 20 TO 30 MINUTES

FOR THE CHOUX PASTRY
¾ cup all-purpose flour
pinch of fine salt
6½ tablespoons unsalted
  butter, diced
3 eggs, lightly beaten
¾ cup slivered almonds

CONTINUED . . .

Pipe (or spoon, if you don't have a pastry bag) large walnut-size ▐
onto the baking sheet(s) in rows, allowing space for the buns-to-
to rise. Sprinkle with the remaining almonds and bake for about
30 minutes until puffed, crisp, and deeply golden. Check after 2(
minutes and reduce the oven temperature slightly if the almonds
browning too much. After 30 minutes, turn the oven off, prop th
door open slightly, and leave the buns inside for another 15 minu
to dry out. Cool on wire racks. It's best to use them immediately
ultimate crispness, but the empty buns can be stored for a day or
two in an airtight tin.

Make the vanilla cream filling. Scrape the seeds from the vanilla
bean with a small knife. In a large bowl, whisk the cream, crème
fraîche, vanilla seeds, confectioners' sugar, and vanilla extract (if
using) together until firm enough to hold its shape.

With a serrated knife, slice each choux bun in half horizontally.
Heap a generous spoonful of vanilla cream onto each lower half ▐
top with a few blueberries. Replace the top halves and, if you fee▐
inclined, dust with confectioners' sugar. Eat soon, before they ha▐
chance to soften too much, with the extra blueberries.

FOR THE VANILLA CREAM
1 plump vanilla bean, split
　　lengthwise
¾ cup heavy cream
¾ cup crème fraîche
scant 1 cup confectioners' sugar,
　　sifted, plus more to dust
a small dash of vanilla extract
　　(optional)
2¾ cups blueberries

Tidal pools

With a bit of luck, these magical windows into the sea will house a teeming variety of sea life. Try to disturb the pools as little as possible as you look and go gently; don't force or break anything. If you have any children with you, they will adore clambering over the rocks at low tide. Take a small net for scooping and have a bucket of sea water ready to keep any tiny fish or shrimp in while you look at them. Be sure to return any creatures and leave everything as you found it.

What you might see under and around the water:

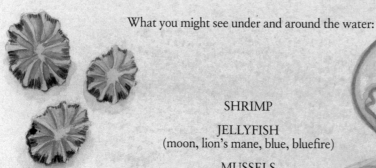

SHRIMP

JELLYFISH
(moon, lion's mane, blue, bluefire)

MUSSELS

CRABS
(most commonly shore crabs but
also porcelain crabs and hermit crabs)

CUTTLEFISH and CUTTLEBONES
(collect them for pet parakeets and lovebirds)

RAZOR SHELLS
(*Ensis ensis*)

GOBY
(common or rock)

STARFISH

TUBE WORMS

PERIWINKLES, LIMPETS,
and BARNACLES

ANEMONES
(green, strawberry, brown, or red forms).
Seen either in "bead" (closed) or open

SEAWEEDS
(lava, dulce, Irish moss, or carageen)

AN EASY, CHIC PICNIC FOR 10

FALL PANZANELLA | GRILLED EGGPLANT AND SUMMER SQUASH *Brik with a roasted tomato sauce* | SESAME COOKIES WITH ICED WATERMELON

Loved by most, but loathed by a notable few, lugging your lunch to that elusive, perfect picnic spot really is worth it. I promise. As long as the heavens don't open. This is definitely a time to watch the forecast closely, and, if the weather fails, there's always a picnic blanket on the living room floor to fall back on. At least then you'll be able to eat with proper flatware, which should please the naysayers.

Guesstimating serving sizes for a large picnic is a precarious game, balancing those content to sit nicely and eat with others who will be more interested in playing Frisbee and dashing about. I work on the premise that one of these main course or hefty salad recipes will serve at least eight, but the whole menu below would actually stretch to ten.

Pack your bounty in Tupperware or light bowls, securely wrapped in plastic. Take lots of napkins and a good, thick blanket. Any dressings or sauces should be carried separately, in lidded jam jars, if adding them too early would result in soggy salads.

Propicnickers, of which I am most certainly one, will know that eating out of doors is magical when you get it right. Granted, the holy grail of locations are mountain tops, forests, fields, and lake sides, but some of my best have been in gardens and parks.

Every year, my friend Tab, who styled the pictures in this book, has a birthday picnic in a secret park in London. She sets up a corner with lovely old bunting and tea lights strung through the trees and everyone brings a dish. Groups of friends turn up through the day and sit on blankets eating, chatting, and occasionally kicking a ball. With just a little effort, she creates something magical. By dusk, the children have gone home and mojitos and birthday cake have appeared for the big kids who remain.

FALL PANZANELLA

SERVES 8 TO 10, AS PART OF A
PICNIC SPREAD
PREP 30 MINUTES
COOK 40 MINUTES

FOR THE SALAD

6 tablespoons olive oil (ideally
   from the artichoke jar), plus
   more for the roasting pans
11 ounces ripe, smallish tomatoes,
   halved
2 tablespoons red wine vinegar
2 red onions, halved and thickly
   sliced through the root
4 mixed red and yellow Romano
   peppers, cut into rough pieces
½ large loaf of day-old
   sourdough, cut into 1¼-inch
   cubes
1 fat garlic clove, crushed
14 ounces char-grilled artichokes
   in oil, drained weight
1 large bunch of basil

FOR THE DRESSING

1 fat garlic clove, crushed
4 tablespoons red wine vinegar
pinch of superfine sugar
6 tablespoons extra-virgin
   olive oil
2 heaping tablespoons capers,
   rinsed well and drained

IF YOU'RE IN THE MARKET FOR SPLURGING, it's well worth getting hold of some of those pricey char-grilled artichoke hearts in oil; one up on the typical antipasti type in jars. Find them in Italian delis, which typically have some nice Apulian ones.

Panzanella benefits from being made a few hours ahead, allowing the bread to soak up the dressing and tomato juices. Take the basil leaves along as a bunch, tearing or slicing the leaves into the salad at the picnic spot.

Preheat the oven to 350°F. Lightly oil a couple of large roasting pans. Arrange the tomatoes in one, cut-sides up, and drizzle with the red wine vinegar, 2 tablespoons oil, and salt and pepper. Toss the red onions, peppers, and 2 tablespoons oil in the other roasting pan. Roast both pans for 35 to 40 minutes, stirring the peppers and onions every now and then but leaving the tomatoes alone. All should be soft and beginning to burn at the edges. Set aside to cool.

Meanwhile, toss the bread with the remaining olive oil and the garlic. Season and roast in the oven for about 15 minutes, turning at least once, until pale golden and crisp. Again, set aside to cool.

Combine the dressing ingredients and season to taste, going easy on the salt because of the capers.

At least 30 minutes, or up to 8 hours, before eating, toss everything together: the peppers and onions, tomatoes, toasted bread, artichokes, and dressing. Don't be gentle; the juices from the roast vegetables need to mingle with the dressing. Add the shredded or torn basil leaves 10 minutes or so before serving and toss again.

GRILLED EGGPLANT AND SUMMER SQUASH

TIME SPENT PEERING OVER THE STOVETOP GRILL PAN, TONGS AT THE READY, IS INEVITABLE HERE. Stovetop grilling thinly sliced vegetables takes a while, simply because there are always so darned many paper-thin slices to cook. Two stovetop grill pans would be the ideal but unrealistic so, failing that, work in batches and be patient. The good news is that all this can be done well ahead of time and smoky ribbons of grilled zucchini and eggplant will a truly stunning salad make.

You can dress this on site (in which case, carry the dressing in a lidded jam jar), or a short while beforehand; take the mozzarella and bunch of mint along separately, ready to add at the last minute.

Start by slicing the zucchini and eggplants lengthwise with a sharp knife, ideally ¾–1¼ inches thick. A sharp swivel peeler works well for the zucchini. Toss the sliced vegetables with the olive oil and season generously.

Place a dry stovetop grill pan over high heat for a few minutes, until smoking hot. Working in small batches, lay vegetable slices out in a single layer, only turning each slice over with tongs when well-marked with dark grill lines (about a minute on each side). As they are ready (when they are marked on both sides), transfer the vegetables to a bowl and continue cooking the rest. If you want to keep the cooled vegetables overnight before making the salad, toss them with a little extra-virgin olive oil before covering and chilling.

To make the dressing, toast the coriander seeds in a dry pan for a minute, until fragrant. Crush lightly in a mortar and pestle or with the underside of a cup. Combine the crushed seeds with the red pepper flakes, honey, lemon zest and juice, extra-virgin olive oil, and seasoning to taste.

No more than 2 hours, or up to a few minutes, before serving, toss the grilled vegetables with the dressing. Just before eating, toss through the mozzarella and the mint.

SERVES 8 AS PART OF A PICNIC SPREAD
PREP 20 MINUTES
COOK 20 MINUTES

FOR THE SALAD
4 zucchini, trimmed
2 large eggplants, trimmed
4 tablespoons olive oil
2 balls buffalo mozzarella, drained and sliced or torn into pieces
1 small bunch of mint, leaves picked and shredded or torn if large

FOR THE DRESSING
1½ tablespoons coriander seeds
good pinch of red pepper flakes
1 tablespoon runny honey
finely grated zest and juice of 1 unwaxed lemon
4 tablespoons, or more, extra-virgin olive oil

HOW SWEET TO BE A CLOUD
Floating in the Blue

Streaky groups of **cirrocumulus**, white and high in the sky, imply the weather will set fair.

Sheets of **cirrostratus** clouds cover the whole sky, only allowing a faint glow of sun or moon to shine through. Cirrostratus usually mean drizzle or even rain will arrive the next day.

Thin and wispy white **cirrus** clouds indicate the weather will stay fair for now, but a change is on its way.

HIGH (16,500–40,00 feet)

Fluffy blankets of gray-white **altocumulus** block out the sun when they pass over it, causing dramatic light and dark effects. A thunderstorm is likely to arrive in a few hours.

Gray or blue-gray **altostratus** block out the sun and the whole sky. A storm is coming.

MIDDLE (6,500–25,000 feet)

Stratus, the drizzle clouds, look like suspended grayish fog. If it is cold enough, the drizzle will fall as light snow.

Cumulonimbus are said to look like giant anvils. The ends of the anvil can point to a rainstorm in the offing.

Beautiful **stratocumulus** lie low in the sky in rows and clumps like herds of fluffy gray sheep. Like sheep they are rather benign; stratocumulus do not bring wet weather with them, but rain could hit when they meet another weather front.

LOW (below 6,500 feet)

Fluffy **cumulus** float over blue skies like clumps of white cotton candy. They bring fair weather, but, if a cumulus starts to grow upward, keep an eye on things; it might get windy and wet later.

Nimbostratus sits in grumpy light gray sheets. Time to sing "rain, rain, go away, come again another day."

VERTICAL (low bases from 16,000 feet and very high tops reaching as high as 49,000 feet)

BRIK
WITH A ROAST TOMATO SAUCE

MAKES 10 OF EACH TYPE
PREP 40 MINUTES PER BATCH
OF 10
COOK 1 HOUR 20 MINUTES
(FETA FILLING) TO 1¾ HOURS
(LAMB FILLING)

FOR THE LAMB FILLING

1¼ pounds lamb neck, trimmed
of excess fat and cut into
2-inch pieces
1 large onion, chopped
1 tablespoon olive oil
11 ounces unpeeled, waxy
potatoes, cut into ½ to ¾-inch
cubes
1 teaspoon cumin seeds
1½ tablespoons capers
large handful of chopped parsley

FOR THE FETA FILLING

2 tablespoons olive oil
1 large red onion, diced
11 ounces unpeeled, waxy
potatoes, cut into ½ to ¾-inch
cubes
1 teaspoon cumin seeds
9 ounces spinach, washed and
any coarse stalks removed
3½ ounces feta, crumbled
½ tablespoon capers
large handful of chopped parsley
no salt!

FOR THE BRIKS

10 tablespoons olive oil
4 eggs, lightly beaten
20 brik pastry sheets or phyllo
dough pastry sheets

BRIK, A CLOSE COUSIN OF THE BÖREK, boureki, bourekas, byrek, and burek (I could go on), is rooted in Algeria and Tunisia. As you can imagine, there are myriad variations, but the main premise of fried or baked pastry enclosing a filling remains true. Traditionally, each brik is fried to order in hot oil until crisp. Gossamer-fine pastry is wrapped around a simple raw filling, including a fresh egg dropped into the center before sealing.

The challenge with picnic food lies in its sitting about; sogginess and greasiness are unwelcome, and that often means fried foods will be suboptimal by the time you come to eat them. In my cheerfully inauthentic version, an egg and olive oil glaze turns the pastry crisp and golden and that crisp quality should hold for a good few hours. Enough time to reach your picnic spot and eat in the sun.

I'd encourage you to crack a small egg into each pastry just before wrapping if you like the idea. I do, and I enjoyed the spoils very much when recipe testing but, in the end, the egg got dropped because more of my willing testers chose the eggless version.

I settled on two fillings, one slow-cooked lamb, suitable for the sharper air of September and, for vegetarians, a feta and spinach version. Both have the bolster of waxy potatoes with capers and cumin to brighten. Play around with them. One of my favorites is a simple mix of diced (raw) red onion, crab, and caper. Brik pastry is available in Turkish stores, but you can just as easily use phyllo dough. I daresay the fillings would work like a charm in a basic pie crust or puff pastry wrapper too.

Preheat the oven to 325°F. For the lamb filling, combine all the ingredients except the capers and parsley in a small roasting pan, season, cover tightly with foil, and cook for 1½ hours or so, until incredibly tender. A fork should meet no real resistance when you use it to roughly shred the lamb. Let cool, stir in the capers and parsley, and adjust the seasoning to taste.

For the vegetarian filling, combine the olive oil, onion, potato, and cumin seeds in a small roasting pan or dish. Cover tightly with foil and roast for 1 hour, at the same temperature as the lamb, until the potatoes are tender. Immediately stir in the spinach and re-cover with foil. Return to the oven for 3 to 5 minutes to wilt the spinach,

CONTINUED...

stir in the remaining ingredients, and set aside to cool. The fillings may be made up to 2 days in advance and kept chilled. Bring up to room temperature before using. When ready to finish the briks, preheat the oven to 350°F. Line 4 large baking sheets with nonstick parchment paper. Whisk the olive oil with the eggs and 2 tablespoons water in a bowl; have a pastry brush at the ready.

Lay a sheet of pastry on a counter, peeling it from its paper backing. Brush lightly with the egg mixture, then lay a heaping tablespoon of your chosen filling in the top right of the circle. Fold the pastry over in half and then again into a quarter to enclose the filling. Brush more egg over the edges and outside, to seal and glaze. Space the briks out on the baking sheets, keeping the side where the filling is more visible facing upward. This is to ensure that the underside crisps up, protected as it is by an extra couple of pastry layers. Repeat to make 10 briks of each type. Bake for 15 minutes, until golden and crisp-edged. Cool on the baking sheets, then pack in layers of wax paper. Transport the sauce (below) in a separate pot.

ROASTED TOMATO SAUCE

MAKES ENOUGH FOR 8 WITH THE BRIKS
PREP 10 MINUTES
COOK 1 HOUR

2¼ pounds ripe tomatoes, halved
pinch of superfine sugar
good drizzle of extra-virgin
   olive oil

THE PANZANELLA RECIPE IN THIS CHAPTER already features roasted tomatoes, cooked at a higher temperature and for less time, but the late-summer bounty is there to be taken advantage of, and this basic sauce is endlessly versatile, ready to be altered as you wish. The long and gentle roasting concentrates the tomato's late-summer flavor enough for it to shine unadorned, but should you wish to enhance it, try whole garlic cloves—added to the roasting pan with their skins on—to be squeezed in after cooking. Herbs such as thyme, oregano, and rosemary torn in beforehand will add depth, as will cumin and coriander seeds, chili, smoked paprika, and even chipotle chilies. Instead of crushing it, puree the sauce if you like, with or without basil or mint. The tomato skins may be removed after cooking for a more refined finish.

Preheat the oven to 300°F. Sit the tomato halves snugly in a roasting pan, cut sides up. Scatter the sugar over with salt and pepper, drizzle generously with olive oil, and roast for 1 hour, until the tomatoes have shriveled slightly. Use a fork or a potato masher to crush the tomatoes down, forming a rustic sauce. Keep, chilled, for up to 5 days. Pack into lidded containers and use as a sauce for the briks (see page 114 and above).

forage for razor clams

FINDING THE CLAMS . . .

When there's a full moon and a new moon, tides sweep out faster and further, exposing swathes of hidden sandy beach that go unseen at other times of the month. Razor clams live around the point of low tide, so larger tides expose their breathing holes and make harvesting far more easy. There are two particularly low tides each year; one falls in mid-March and the other in mid-September. If at all possible, go clamming when these tides fall; your chances of success will be at their highest.

Look up the tide times and go to the beach when the tide is almost at its lowest. Take a tub of fine salt, the everyday "table" sort with a small dispenser in the top. Step quietly and leave the dog at home; the clams will quickly retract if they sense a disturbance.

Working along the sand near the water, look for the breathing holes, which will be smaller than a quarter and elongated rather than round. Sometimes the holes will "foam" as the clam breathes. Pour salt into the hole and wait for a few seconds. The clam should push up to the surface because he thinks the briny tide is coming in. Be patient and wait until he is exposed by at least a thumb's length before you strike. Grasp the clam and pull firmly but slowly, easing it from the sand.

As you go, put the clams into a bucket of clean sea water to help purge any sand out. Don't keep them in this water for longer than an hour or so, though, or they might drown.

If you buy your clams from a fishmonger, they will be cleaned already. Make sure they smell pleasantly of the sea, rather than at all fishy,

and that the flesh is whitish and plump, not discolored with brownish tinges.

. . . AND PREPARING THEM

Like squid, clams are easy to overcook, so go cautiously to get the best from their sweet flesh. Eat as soon as you can, but they keep overnight, wrapped in wet newspaper and well-chilled.

The possibilities are varied and if you're looking for something different, razor clams make a beautiful ceviche. Three or four each will do as an appetizer, six to eight as a main course.

The easiest way for novices to prepare them is: Soak in cool, unsalted water for thirty minutes, then rinse. This is to remove as much sand as possible. Grill or steam in their shells for a minute or so, just enough to open them. Let cool a little before taking the flesh out and cutting off the digger (the black end). If the clams look sandy, rinse again. In bad cases, you can snip along the length of the clam, rinsing sand away as you go.

To grill them (the simplest way), return them to the shells and grill until firm and just opaque.

Serve with garlic butter, or sizzled chorizo and its oil with parsley. Vietnamese-style dressings of fish sauce, sugar, lime juice and minced chili, spooned over the steamed flesh, are also excellent.

You can also treat the razor clams like mussels, adding them to a buttery mix of softened shallot and garlic, then pouring in white wine and covering until cooked. Chopped parsley and an optional splash of cream will top things off nicely.

RAZOR SHELLS *(Ensis ensis), or razor clams, or razor fish, are sand-burrowing bivalves. They grow to 5–8 inches long and, with their curved, brownish shells, resemble an old barber's blade. If you can get to a beach that is sandy at low tide, it is worth foraging for razor clams; they are as delightful as scallops and it's fun.*

SESAME COOKIES WITH ICED WATERMELON

MAKES AROUND 25 COOKIES
PREP 20 MINUTES
COOK 12 MINUTES

scant ½ cup unsalted butter,
    softened
¾ cup light or dark brown sugar
1 egg
8 tablespoon light sesame seed
    (tahini) paste
1 teaspoon vanilla extract
pinch of salt
scant 1½ cups all-purpose flour
1 teaspoon baking soda
generous ⅓ cup sesame seeds
2 tablespoons raw brown sugar

THE ICED WATERMELON INVOLVES NOTHING MORE FANCY THAN A BOWLING BALL-SIZE, whole watermelon, thoroughly chilled overnight. Take a knife and a bag of ice along to sit the sliced melon on, stealing a few cubes to keep drinks cool. Soft-crumbed cookies are a lovely way to use up the jar of sesame seed paste that sits around between sporadic bouts of hummus-making. Use 1 tablespoon less butter and add a tablespoon of toasted sesame oil in its place if you particularly love sesame. Dark brown sugar will garner moodier results than light. I have also had much success substituting peanut butter for the sesame seed paste and finely chopped peanuts for sesame seeds, so I'm quite sure any nut butter and its matching nut would work too. Last on the variation advice, ground ginger and/or cinnamon make warming additions in the colder months.

Preheat the oven to 350°F. Line two large baking sheets with nonstick parchment paper.

Using electric beaters, or a wooden spoon and elbow grease, beat the butter and sugar together until light, followed by the egg. Follow with the sesame seed paste, a tablespoon at a time as you beat, then the vanilla extract and salt.

Sift the flour and baking soda over, followed by a tablespoon of the sesame seeds, and mix with a wooden spoon until combined.

Empty the remaining sesame seeds onto a plate with the raw brown sugar. Roll heaping teaspoons of the dough into spheres, then roll these firmly in the sesame-sugar plate. Space well apart on the baking sheets and cook for 10 to 12 minutes, until pale golden. Let firm up on the baking sheets for a couple of minutes, then transfer to wire racks to cool completely.

HARVEST FESTIVAL LUNCH FOR 8

CRISP HAM HOCK AND PUMPKIN SALAD, CHILI DRESSING, AND TOASTED PUMPKIN SEEDS
CHICKEN AND WILD MUSHROOM PIES WITH BUTTERED KALE | *Black grape jelly with muscat sabayon*

If there was ever a time to shop at farmers' markets, farm stores, and local grocery stores, this is the season to do it. Mid- to late-fall's produce stalls spill forth with ruddy, russet-skinned fruits and tactile gourds. It is now, rather than amid spring's deluge of new growth, that the soil and the changing seasons can be felt most keenly. Cooking for large numbers is easy when there is so much good—and cheap—bounty to be found. And we are spoiled by the choices. From Jerusalem artichokes, wild mushrooms, and truffles to perfumed grapes in dripping bunches and the last of the buxom figs, splitting under their own weight, a need to harvest, to stock up for the cold to come, looms large.

All of a sudden, it is okay to spend a weekend afternoon puttering in the kitchen, making a stew for later or baking a cake. Earlier in the fall—and especially during a late Indian summer—it feels like a waste of summer's remnants to spend any more time indoors than is necessary. The arrival of cold mornings and dark evenings brings with them a twinge of sad relief. Summer is done with for another year and winter creeps in to take her place.

A warming, late lunch is ideal for a fall weekend. Hopefully, the day will be suited to a golden morning walk through turning leaves. Thankfully, a chicken pie will be just as welcome on gray-skied and damp days, which depending on your climate may be the more likely scenario. The recipes should allow time off for good behavior, for much can be made in advance. The grape jellies and their sabayon, the components of the salad and the chicken pies can all be done a day, or two days, ahead. The morning's cooking should then consist of mere assembly jobs: rewarming the ham for the salad before jumbling everything together to eat; baking the pies; and wilting a mound of buttery greens.

CRISP HAM HOCK AND PUMPKIN SALAD,
CHILI DRESSING, AND TOASTED PUMPKIN SEEDS

THIS RAMBUNCTIOUS SALAD happens to be one of my very favorite recipes in the book. Normally, I try to take the authentic route with Asian dishes, but mild olive oil and pumpkin seeds make for such a harmonious marriage with chili, ginger, and kaffir lime that, in this case, I don't think authenticity matters a jot.

All too often, ham is cured in overly salty brines. Remedy this by soaking the hocks in cool water for a few hours before cooking, changing the water as and when you remember.

Preheat the oven to 325°F. Put the ham hocks into a small roasting pan and cover with foil. Cook for 2 hours or so, until almost falling apart. Cool until you can strip away the fat and skin, tearing the meat into large pieces. (This may be done up to 2 days in advance. Return to room temperature for 15 minutes or so, then place in a roasting pan, cover with foil, and reheat in a low oven.) Increase the oven temperature to 425°F. Toss the pumpkin with the oil, season generously, and roast on a lined baking sheet for about 30 minutes, until golden at the edges and tender. Let cool slightly. (Again, this can be done up to 2 days beforehand. Return to room temperature before using.)

Onto the dressing. To prepare the lime leaves, stack them on top of each other and roll up tightly. Slice very, very finely to get whisper-thin shreds, avoiding the stalk (throw that bit away). Place 4 tablespoons of the oil in a skillet and add the shallots. Cook gently, stirring often, for about 10 minutes. They should look shriveled but not deeply colored. Now add the sugar and stir for 2 minutes. Follow with the chilies, ginger, garlic, lemongrass, and lime leaves, keeping the heat very low and cooking for another 5 minutes. Remove from the heat and let cool slightly. Stir in the soy sauce, lime juice, remaining olive oil, and the sesame oil.

Toast the pumpkin seeds in a dry skillet, shaking them about until puffed and fragrant. Set aside to cool. To serve, combine the salad and herb leaves in a large bowl, scatter the pumpkin, avocado, and ham over, followed by the dressing and a twist of black pepper. Fluff everything up a bit and shower with pumpkin seeds. Take to the table for everyone to serve themselves.

SERVES 8
PREP 40 MINUTES
COOK 2 HOURS 50 MINUTES

FOR THE SALAD
3 smoked ham hocks
2 pounds pumpkin or squash, peeled if the skin is very tough, and sliced ³/₄–1¹/₄ inches thick
2 tablespoons olive oil
³/₄ cup pumpkin seeds
2 large handfuls of characterful mixed leaves (mizuna, arugula, chard, young spinach)
generous handful of cilantro leaves
handful of Thai basil leaves (or more cilantro if you can't find it)
2 large, ripe avocados, cut into thin segments

FOR THE DRESSING
4 kaffir lime leaves
6 tablespoons mild olive oil
3 shallots, very finely sliced
scant ¹/₄ cup palm sugar or 3 tablespoons light brown sugar
2 red chilies, very finely sliced
thumb-size piece of fresh gingerroot, peeled and sliced into fine thin sticks
1 fat garlic clove, minced
2 lemongrass stalks, trimmed and finely sliced
3 tablespoons soy sauce
juice of 1 lime
1 teaspoon toasted sesame oil

CHICKEN AND WILD MUSHROOM PIES
WITH BUTTERED KALE

**MAKES 8 INDIVIDUAL PIES,
OR 2 4-PERSON PIES**
PREP 2 HOURS
COOK ABOUT 1½ HOURS

FOR THE PIE DOUGH

2 cups (4 sticks) unsalted butter,
chilled and cubed
generous 6¾ cups all-purpose
flour, plus more to dust
2 teaspoons salt

FOR THE POACHED CHICKEN

3¼ pounds whole free-range
chicken
1 large onion, halved
1 large leek, roughly chopped
2 large carrots, roughly chopped
2 tablespoons dried mushrooms
bouquet garni of 2 bay leaves
with a few sprigs of parsley
and thyme

FOR THE FILLING

¾ cup white wine
⅔ cup light cream
6 tablespoons unsalted butter,
cubed
½ cup all-purpose flour
2 tablespoons chopped parsley,
or 1 tablespoon chopped
tarragon

THESE ARE PIES TO GLADDEN THE HEART: woodsy mushrooms, gently poached chicken, and a sauce that really tastes of the latter, rather than of cream or stock cubes. Use eight 2-cup pie dishes or ovenproof bowls, or two 8-inch pie dishes for larger pies. If you can't afford wild, use cremini and portobello mushrooms and give the flavor a boost with a few dried porcini, soaked and chopped.

Start by making the pie dough. I find it easiest to divide the ingredients in half to make two batches (such is the life of the mass caterer). Using the pulse button, whizz half the butter, half the flour, and half the salt for a couple of minutes, until it looks like coarse sand. Tip into a bowl and, using a table knife, cut in just enough ice water (around 2–3 tablespoons) to get the mixture clumping together. Tip onto a counter and lightly bring together into a ball. Flatten to form a round and wrap in plastic wrap. Repeat to make a second round and chill both for at least 1 hour, or up to 3 days.

Sit the chicken, onion, leek, carrots, dried mushrooms, and bouquet garni in a large casserole or pan; it should be snug, but not too snug, and have a bit of space above it. Cover with cool water by ¾ inch, then bring to a boil. Skim off any foam, then reduce the heat so far down the water barely sputters. Let the chicken poach for an hour, then turn the heat off and let the bird cool in the stock. Lift the chicken out of the stock and set aside. Skim any fat from the surface, then strain the stock. As soon it is cool enough to handle, remove the meat from the chicken, flaking it into large chunks in a bowl; chucking out all the skin, fat, gristle, and bones as you go.

Measure 4 cups of the strained stock into a pan—freeze the rest for soups and sauces—add the wine and reduce over high heat, until only half its volume remains. Stir in the cream, taste, and adjust the seasoning. Keep the liquid hot for the next stage . . .

To make the sauce, melt the butter in a large pan, stir in the flour, and cook, stirring constantly, for a couple of minutes. Swap to a balloon whisk and slowly begin to add the hot, reduced stock, whisking constantly. Keep adding and whisking to make a thick sauce. Bring to a simmer and whisk for 5 minutes to get rid of any "floury" taste. Season lightly and add the herbs.

CONTINUED . . .

FOR THE MUSHROOMS

1 tablespoon olive oil

1 tablespoon unsalted butter

1 pound 2 ounces mixed wild
mushrooms, brushed and torn
into bits

1 fat garlic clove, crushed
(optional)

FOR THE GLAZE

2 egg yolks, lightly beaten

2 tablespoons milk

Heat the olive oil and butter for the mushrooms in your largest
skillet. Sauté the mushrooms briskly, stirring sparingly, for a few
minutes, until browned in places and wilted; any liquid should ha
evaporated. If you are adding the garlic, add it in a couple of min
before removing from the heat. Season, then add to the shredded
chicken. Pour the sauce over and gently mix. Cover and chill for
to 48 hours, or use immediately.

Preheat the oven to 375°F. Depending on the size of your oven,
one large or two medium baking sheets in to preheat. Remove th
pie dough from the refrigerator about 30 minutes before needed.
Cut out 6½- by 1¼-inch strips of parchment paper or foil, two p
small pie dish, laid in as a cross with the ends sticking out of the
dish. This will enable you to lift the cooked pies out easily.

On a lightly floured counter, roll the first round of pie dough out
the thickness of ⅛ inch. Use it to line the pie dishes (make sure t
ends of the paper strips are still visible), leaving an overhang. Fill
each dish with chicken, right to the top. Repeat with the second
round of pie dough. Beat the egg yolk and milk together. Using a
pastry brush, paint this around the rim of each pie then cut a lid a
lay it over, pressing down firmly. Cut away the excess pastry and
crimp the edges or press with the tines of a fork. Brush the glaze
over the pies and cut a hole in the tops to release steam.

Slide them onto the preheated baking sheet(s) and cook for 50
minutes to 1 hour, until deeply burnished. Cover them with foil if
they brown too quickly. Let the cooked pies rest for a few minute
Carefully lift from their dishes using the paper strips. (Or cut heft
slices from a large pie.) Serve with Buttered Kale (see below).

BUTTERED KALE

BUTTERED BLACK KALE WOULD BE A MORE ACCURA
TITLE, but it felt somewhat cumbersome and a touch dictatorial
when there are plenty of other kales in the running.

SERVES 8
PREP 10 MINUTES
COOK 5 MINUTES OR SO

3 bunches of cavolo nero or
other kale or greens

2 generous pieces of unsalted
butter

dash of olive oil

2 garlic cloves, very finely sliced

good grating of nutmeg

Wash the kale thoroughly and drain well. Trim away the tough
central stalks and chop the leaves, if large.

Melt the butter with a little olive oil, to prevent it burning. When
all is foaming nicely, add the garlic and cook for a minute or so.
Now add the kale, turning over to coat in the butter. Cook, stirrir
now and then, until wilted. Season generously with salt and pepp
finishing with a generous grating of nutmeg.

≥APPLES≤

Worcester Pearmain delicately blushed pink early apple with a hint of strawberry flavor

Laxton's Superb a late Victorian dessert apple with a firm texture and sweet taste

Bramley's Seedling the UK's favorite cooking apple has a sharp, acidic taste when raw. However, it cooks down to a beautifully smooth, balanced puree

Egremont Russet crisp when freshly picked, with a good balance of sweetness and acidity

Cox's Orange Pippin a very well-known apple with an orange-red hue, an intense but sweet flavor and a crisp texture

Blenheim Orange primarily grown as a cooking apple, when it forms a firm puree, this also has good eating properties, especially with cheese

WINTER SQUASH & *Pumpkins*

Honey Bear an acorn squash variety with deep green skin and firm orange flesh. Ideal to bake, stuff, or make soup with

Butternut squash or butternut pumpkin, has sweet, firm, orange flesh. Roasts beautifully

Baby Bear mini pumpkin that makes an ideal single serving and roasts well to eat as is, or forms a good, edible soup bowl

Crown Prince gorgeous blue-gray-green skin and intense orange flesh which roasts and purees exceptionally

Spaghetti squash steam or bake with butter and cheese, then tease out the light, spaghetti-like flesh and serve as "pasta"

Festival squash lovely, striped, and speckled skin. The sweet orange flesh is ideal for baking or stuffing

BLACK GRAPE JELLY WITH MUSCAT SABAYON

MAKES 8 JELLIES AND ANOUGH SABAYON FOR EACH
PREP 20 MINUTES, PLUS AT LEAST 5 HOURS CHILLING
COOK ABOUT 15 MINUTES

FOR THE JELLIES

4 tablespoons superfine sugar
5 cups chilled black or red grape juice
14 gelatin leaves or 4½ teaspoons gelatin granules
¾ cup sweet muscat wine
small bunch of black grapes, halved, to serve (optional)

FOR THE SABAYON

6 egg yolks
scant ½ cup sweet muscat wine
4 tablespoons superfine sugar
¾ cup heavy cream, lightly whipped

THIS IS A DESSERT TO PREPARE COMPLETELY AHEAD OF TIME. The jellies can be made a day or so in advance and the sabayon on the night before, or, ideally, first thing in the morning. You only have to spoon the chilled sabayon over the none-too-sweet jellies before eating.

Organic grape juice is a beauty. It's deep and dark and clear and leaves you with handsome glass bottles once the juice has gone. Do, of course, juice your own grapes should you have a glut of beauties on your hands (in which case, I'm incredibly jealous); otherwise, a good-quality, store-bought juice will be fine and dandy. A sweet muscat with its notes of orange blossom goes into both sabayon and jelly, but you could use any sweet wine you have to hand. A Tokaji, perhaps?

Accompany with some crisp or shortbread-y cookies, if you wish, but I am taken by this cool jelly and feather-light sabayon unsullied and unchaperoned.

Start with the jellies. In a pan set over low heat, warm the sugar in scant ½ cup of the grape juice and ¾ cup water, until dissolved and steaming but not boiling. Meanwhile, soak the gelatin leaves (if using) in cold water for 3 minutes until soft. Squeeze the water out with your hands and stir into the hot juice until completely melted. (If you are using gelatin granules or powder, sprinkle evenly over the panful of hot juice and stir to dissolve.) Gradually add the remaining cold grape juice and the wine, stirring as you do so. Pour into 8 small (about ¾-cup capacity) serving bowls or cups and let cool completely; then cover and refrigerate for at least 5 hours or overnight to set.

To make the sabayon, whisk the egg yolks, 2 tablespoons of the muscat, and all of the sugar in a heatproof bowl set over, but not touching, a pan of simmering water. I use a handheld electric whisk for this, but it's perfectly possible with an arm-powered one. Keep whisking for about 10 minutes, until the mixture is thick and pale in color. Remove from the heat and whisk in the remaining muscat, followed by the cream. Whisk briefly every now and then as the mixture cools, then cover and chill for up to 4 hours, until needed. Serve the jellies and sabayon with the halved grapes, if you like.

FIREPIT NIGHT FOR 8 TO 10

MELTED RACLETTE BOWLS WITH PUMPKIN SALSA | *Olive pressers' soup*
AFTER FIREWORKS AND FIREPITS: STUFFED FIREPIT VENISON WITH ROASTED PEAR, PORT SAUCE, AND PERFECT MASHED POTATOES
HOT PEAR AND RUM PUNCH | STICKY DATE AND GINGER CAKE

No late-fall revelry is complete without a bonfire, but if you have an area of garden or field in which to build a firepit, you will benefit from both outdoor fire and oven in one.

Building, and cooking in, the pit is incredibly rewarding, and it's pretty easy to construct, despite requiring some work with a shovel. Quite apart from the theater and fun of it all, the firepit imbues the meat, fish, and vegetables cooked in it with a smoky note, rendering them juicy and tender. (Detailed instructions on building the pit can be found on pages 140–141.) Gather a group to share the digging—nothing wrong with working for your supper—and you'll have a pit that can be used time and again. If you are nervous about cooking underground, dig the pit a few days beforehand and have a trial run with a leg of lamb. If you err on the side of gentle the first time (definitely preferable to overzealous heat), the meat can always be finished off in a low oven. Rain on the night won't be a problem as long as it starts after supper has been buried.

In its entirety, this celebratory menu will serve eight so very generously that I encourage you to keep the quantities the same for ten guests. If making one of the recipes on its own, plan on it serving eight. Whatever the numbers, there is far too much food here to constitute supper in one sitting. It's a real feast, and one that can be prepared in stages, starting a few days ahead. The raclette and soup are intended as an early evening refuel, once the pit has been dug and lit. The fire can burn down to embers while you eat. Bury the venison and let it cook as you marvel at fireworks, light some sparklers, and enjoy the party for a couple of hours, then uncover the firepit in time for a late supper.

MELTED RACLETTE BOWLS WITH
PUMPKIN SALSA

THIS IS GLORIOUSLY EASY FOOD FOR A CROWD if you make the sweet-salty-sour salsa in advance (up to three days ahead is fine). Should the cheese cool down too much to scoop while you're eating, putting the bowls back into the oven for a few minutes will restore them to molten goodness.

Preheat the oven to 400°F. Divide the peppers, pumpkin, and about one-quarter of the oregano between two roasting trays and douse each pile with a little oil to coat, saving at least 2 tablespoons for the finished salsa. Season generously and roast for 50 minutes, until browned and sticky. Set aside to cool.

Toast the pine nuts in a dry skillet, shaking often, until golden. Combine with the pumpkin mixture and the remaining salsa ingredients, including the remaining oil and oregano, and season well. Taste; the flavors should be bouncy and pronounced, so add a splash more vinegar and/or more black pepper if you feel it needs it. You can make this a couple of days in advance and keep it in the refrigerator; return to room temperature before eating.

Reduce the oven temperature to 375°F. Slice the cheese thickly—rind and all—and divide between about four ovenproof bowls or dishes. Cook for 8 to 10 minutes, until the cheese is melted and bubbling at the edges. Spoon the salsa straight onto each bowl of cheese and serve with the breads for dipping and scooping. You might want to warn people, restaurant-style, that the bowls will be hot.

SERVES 8 TO 10
PREP 20 MINUTES
COOK ABOUT 1 HOUR

FOR THE SALSA
2 yellow and 2 orange bell
    peppers, seeded and diced
1¼ pounds firm-fleshed pumpkin
    or squash, peeled, seeded,
    and finely diced
leaves from 4 sprigs of oregano,
    chopped
about 6 tablespoons extra-virgin
    olive oil
3 tablespoons pine nuts
splash of good balsamic vinegar,
    or to taste
¼ cup green olives, pitted and
    roughly chopped
1 small garlic clove, crushed

FOR THE RACLETTE BOWLS
1¾ pounds raclette cheese
rustic Italian breads or
    flatbreads, to serve

OLIVE PRESSERS' SOUP

SERVES 8 TO **10**
PREP 30 MINUTES, PLUS
    OVERNIGHT SOAKING IF USING
    DRIED BEANS
COOK ABOUT 2½ HOURS, IF USING
    DRIED BEANS

2¼ cups dried haricot or
    cranberry beans, or 3 14-ounce
    cans of the same, drained
bouquet garni of fresh bay,
    thyme, and rosemary
3½ ounces smoked bacon cubes
    (optional)
1 tablespoon olive oil (optional)
1½ pounds kale or savoy
    cabbage
11 ounces firm-fleshed pumpkin
    or squash, peeled and diced
1 large carrot, scrubbed
    and diced
1 fennel bulb, trimmed and diced,
    fronds set aside and chopped
1 celery stalk, sliced
4 potatoes, diced
generous handful of mixed soft
    herbs, roughly chopped
extra-virgin olive oil
1 tablespoon tomato paste
8-10 thick slices of rustic bread
1 garlic clove, halved

A SOUP FOR OLIVE GATHERING AND PRESSING, WINTRY WALKS, or for rewarding sterling pit-digging efforts. This is a sturdy, ribollita-like affair, not blessed with stunning looks but far more distinguished than its humble ingredients would suggest. Cook it two or three days in advance to make life simpler, and to deepen the soup's character. When it comes to herbs, I use a mixture of basil and parsley with a touch of sage and thyme. Use whatever you have on hand, but go easy with the more dominant, woody herbs. Obviously, leave out the bacon to make this suitable for vegetarians. I make no apology for using pumpkin or squash twice in one menu; seasonal ingredients are there to be celebrated, and one large pumpkin or squash will provide for both salsa and soup.

If you are using dried beans—and it is worth the extra fuss—soak them overnight in plenty of cool water. Drain, rinse, and drain again. In a large pan, generously cover the beans with cold water, add the bouquet garni, and bring to a boil, skimming off any scum that rises to the surface. Cover and simmer for 1 to 1½ hours, or until tender. This very much depends on the age of your beans and the soaking time, so be prepared to test after 40 minutes or cook them for far longer. Remove one-third of the cooked beans with a slotted spoon and set aside for a later stage.

In another large pan, fry the bacon in the oil (if using) until browned. Add the beans (not the reserved third) and their liquid, the kale, pumpkin, carrot, fennel bulb and fronds, celery, potatoes, herbs, glug of extra-virgin olive oil, tomato paste, and seasoning. Add enough extra water, if needed, to cover the ingredients by ¾ inch.

Bring to a boil, partially cover and simmer for 1½ hours, stirring now and then, until the beans begin to break down. Add the reserved beans and turn off the heat. The texture should be very thick, but do add a little more water if you feel the soup needs it. At this stage the soup can be cooled and chilled for up to 3 days.

Toast or griddle the bread until very well colored, even charred in places. Rub each surface with the cut sides of the garlic clove.

Divide the toast between warmed bowls, sprinkle with extra-virgin olive oil, and ladle the soup over. Serve immediately or cover each bowl with foil and leave in a warm (not hot!) oven for 30 minutes.

STUFFED FIREPIT VENISON
WITH ROASTED PEAR, PORT SAUCE, AND PERFECT MASHED POTATOES

FOR ITS SHEER SIZE, A LARGE LEG OF VENISON IS A PRETTY GOOD BUY; taking quality and sustainability of venison into account, the value is excellent and will allow you to feed a large crowd with style. For safety, please use a meat thermometer after cooking, especially with a firepit, inserting it into the thickest part and waiting for 20 seconds. It should read 122°F for rare, 140°F for medium-rare (158°F upward is well done); though a couple of degrees either side is fine.

For the stuffing, gently fry the onion in the butter for 10 minutes, until soft and beginning to color. Add the garlic, pears, and herbs and cook for 5 minutes more. Remove from the heat and stir in the bread crumbs, walnuts, and lemon zest with plenty of seasoning. Stir in the egg after a few minutes, when the stuffing has cooled slightly. Cover and chill. Return to room temperature before using.

To make the sauce, use a large pan to fry the shallots or red onion in the oil and half the butter for 10 to 15 minutes, stirring often, until very soft and turning golden. Now add the rosemary and port, bring up to a brisk boil, and cook until reduced by half. Add the stock and boil again, until the sauce has reduced by two-thirds. Taste and season if needed, it should be slightly syrupy. Cool, cover, and chill for up to 3 days. Reheat gently when needed, whisking the remaining cubes of butter in one by one until the sauce is shiny.

Open the venison out on a board and spoon the stuffing down the center. Roll the stuffed venison as tightly as possible from one long side, to enclose the stuffing and make a fat sausage. Tie in place firmly and at even intervals, with about eight lengths of string. Arrange the prosciutto in a large rectangle of overlapping slices, sit the venison on one edge, and roll up in the ham. Now lay out a large sheet of parchment paper and put the sage on top. Sit the venison on top of this and wrap up tightly, twisting the ends like a candy wrapper.

This is where it is sensible to move the operation outside, near to a hose or outdoor faucet. Take a couple of sections of last weekend's broadsheet newspaper, separate them into layers of two or three pages, and soak them—and I mean thoroughly soak—with water. Wrap each wetted layer around the venison, finishing with a further slosh of water. If you have followed the firepit instructions on pages 140–141, the embers should be white and ashen and glowing in places, with no hint

SERVES 8 TO **10**
PREP 1½ HOURS
COOK 2½ HOURS, PLUS RESTING

FOR THE STUFFING
1 large red onion, chopped
6 tablespoons unsalted butter
3 garlic cloves, minced
3 pears, cored and diced
2 tablespoons minced rosemary leaves
5 sage leaves, shredded
scant 2 cups white bread crumbs
½ cup walnuts, chopped
finely grated zest of 1 lemon
1 egg, beaten

FOR THE PORT SAUCE
14 ounces shallots or red onion, finely sliced
1 tablespoon olive oil
generous ¼ cup unsalted butter, chilled and diced
1 large sprig of rosemary
3⅓ cups port
4 cups good brown beef or chicken stock

FOR THE VENISON
6½ pounds leg of venison, boned out
18 slices prosciutto
bunch of sage

FOR THE ROAST PEARS
6 firm Bartlett pears
handful of sprigs of rosemary
4 tablespoons unsalted butter, softened

CONTINUED . . .

of flame. Carefully place your wet logs on the coals and cover with the metal grate. Lay the venison package on this, balance the sheet of metal above and cover with earth as directed.

Let cook for 1 hour 25 minutes for a 6½-pound joint (that's 14 minutes per 1 pound 2 ounces, allowing for 10 minutes' digging time). With any luck, the meat will be medium-rare. Then, wearing protective gloves, dig up and retrieve the venison to much applause.

If you have a meat thermometer, stick it into the venison now and leave for 20 seconds. It should read around 140°F. (See the recipe introduction for more detailed temperatures.)

NO FIREPIT?

If you don't have room for a firepit, worry not. You can use a Weber-style barbecue, or this recipe will be as successful, albeit a little less smoky, when cooked in a hot oven. To do this, lay the stuffed and ham-swaddled venison in your largest, oiled roasting pan, tuck in just a few sage leaves, and cover with buttered foil. Roast in a preheated oven at 325°F for 14 minutes per 1 pound 2 ounces for medium rare (that's basically 1 hour 25 minutes for a 6½-pound joint). A joint this size will need an extra 20 minute blast at a higher temperature. To do this, remove the foil and increase the oven temperature to 400°F. Rest the meat for a good 20 minutes, tented with foil, before slicing.

Meanwhile, preheat the oven to 400°F. Slice the pears into sixths, from top to bottom, removing any core as you go. Spread out in a single layer in a roasting pan with the rosemary and butter. Season lightly and roast for 20 minutes, or until softened and turning golden.

Slice the venison thickly, being careful to cut through and remove all the string as you go. Serve the venison slices with Perfect Mashed Potatoes (see right), the port sauce, and two or three elegant roast pear pieces.

PERFECT MASHED POTATOES FOR A CROWD

SERVES 8 TO **10 WITH THE VENISON**
PREP 25 MINUTES
COOK ABOUT 25 MINUTES

A TRICK WHEN MAKING MASHED POTATOES (OR OTHER VEGETABLES) FOR LARGE NUMBERS: on the morning of your party, make the mash, then, when needed, reheat until browned on top and spoon straight from the dish. Ricing potatoes—and I do strongly recommend this over mashing, if you can get hold of a cheap ricer—for ten at the last minute is to be avoided if possible and the crisp, golden top will be delicious. Choose even-size, not large, spuds so that they cook at the same time.

Cover the whole potatoes with water in a very large pan (you may need two pans), add a pinch of salt, and bring to a boil. Simmer for 20 to 25 minutes, until the potatoes are completely tender but not collapsing. Drain thoroughly and let cool for a few minutes. As soon as you can bear to, peel or pare the skin away.

Working in batches, push the potatoes through a potato ricer into a mixing bowl. Slowly beat in the milk or cream with a wooden spoon. Add scant ½ to 1 cup butter, to taste—the amount is totally up to you—beating it in a few cubes at a time, until all is amalgamated. Season with salt and pepper. Spoon, or even pipe, if you're that way inclined, the finished mash into a baking dish and dot with the remaining 3 tablespoons of butter. Keep in a cool place until needed.

Reheat the potatoes for 25 minutes at 400°F when you cook the Roast Pears (see left). The top should be burnished and golden.

FOR THE MASH

2¾ pounds medium mealy potatoes

1½ cups whole milk or light cream, hot but not boiling

generous ½-1 cup unsalted butter, chilled and diced small, to taste

HOT PEAR AND RUM PUNCH

SERVES 8 TO **10**
PREP 5 MINUTES
COOK ABOUT 10 MINUTES

KEEP THE HEAT LOW TO PREVENT THE ALCOHOL BURNING OFF, and do add rum to taste rather than adhering to a measurement. The kitchen will smell like Christmas after making this.

Heat, but don't boil, all the ingredients together in a large pan for about 10 minutes. Serve hot.

4 tablespoons maple syrup

2 cinnamon sticks

4 cloves

6 allspice berries

zest of 1 orange and 1 unwaxed lemon

8 cups fresh pear juice

¼ cup rum, or to taste

Have no illusions, building a firepit is certainly a fun and rewarding weekend project, but the digging part is extremely hard work. I find a pit most suited to cooking large joints of meat, so I reference that here, but you can also use it to cook vegetables; whole potatoes and roots are a good choice. They should be wrapped in layers of foil, with a few herb sprigs enclosed.

WHAT YOU WILL NEED

At least one spade

At least 9 bricks or 4 cinder blocks

A metal rack from a barbecue or similar, no bigger than 31½ by 14¾-17¾ inches in diameter

A bucket of water

Matches

Kindling to start the fire

At least a wheelbarrowful of logs to burn

A rake

A few small cherry or apple wood logs, submerged in cool water for a few hours

Protective gloves

A sturdy sheet of metal, about 31½ by 14¾ inches

A thick, old blanket or mat

A tarpaulin to cover the pit if it rains before it is dug out

First, find a suitable piece of private ground that you have permission to dig up. It should be grass or earth—not rocky—flat, dry, and away from overhanging trees.

DIGGING THE PIT

You're going to expend quite a bit of energy here, probably an hour or two's worth, so assemble your crack team of workers. My talents seem to lie in a bit of a dig, followed by a predominantly supervising-slash-directing role. Yours may differ. Working in a rough rectangle of around 3 foot by 20 inches, take the top layer of turf off in long, shallow strips, using a sharp spade. Roll the turf strips up, soil-side out, and set aside somewhere sheltered where they won't dry out, where they are ready to replace later.

Dig down to a depth of about 20 inches, piling the earth up close because you'll need it again later.

Working in the base of the pit, either mound up a bit of firm earth at either end, or place pairs of stacked-up bricks or a cinder block at each end instead. Balance the metal rack on top, so that it sits about 12 inches above the base of the pit. Any closer and the food will scorch. Remove the rack and set aside, leaving the earth or bricks in place.

THE FIRE

Dampen any grass around the edge of the pit with water and remove any long-dried-out plant life that could catch fire.

Use dry sticks and twigs as kindling to get a flame going, gradually building the fire up with bigger pieces of wood, until at least a barrow load of dry logs is burning. Over the next couple of hours, you want the logs to burn down slowly, forming a thick layer of dusty-looking, white-hot embers. This is a very important step if your firepit is to retain enough heat to cook meat through gently but adequately. There mustn't be any flames in the pit when you start to cook, or the meat will scorch before it has cooked through.

Sparks may fly out, so keep extra firewood at a safe distance and have the bucket of water on hand to dampen down any dry grass, if necessary.

WRAPPING THE MEAT

Soak at least eight sheets of broadsheet newspaper very thoroughly in water. Tuck any aromatics, such as herbs, whole spices, or citrus zests in with the meat, then wrap it in parchment paper and then in the wet newspaper layers, which should prevent scorching.

If the meat is very juicy—a boned shoulder of pork or a whole chicken, for example—I will wrap the lot in a double-layer of foil; it offers extra protection and keeps the cooking juices in. The package will gently smoke and cook underground for a couple of hours to many hours, depending on size and type, so I tend to dig the firepit one day, keeping the hole covered with a tarpaulin if it rains. Starting the fire the following day will mean the feast will be ready that evening, but you could just as easily do the lot in a single day. Joints of meat that have a rich marbling of fat to prevent them drying out should not suffer from some extra hours of cooking, so go for large shoulders and legs, rather than lean cuts.

CREATING SMOKE AND COOKING

When the logs are ready, rake them out a little to form an even layer. Lay a few soaked cherry or apple wood logs on top of the fire. Wear protective gloves to carefully lower the rack down until it rests in position above the embers and smoking logs. Sit a couple of bricks or a cinder block at either end of the rack.

Lay your well-wrapped meat on the grill and balance the sturdy metal sheet over it. The metal should just fit snugly into the hole, if possible.

Re-cover everything with the dug out soil, making sure that there are no holes for the heat to escape through. Cover the earth mound with an old blanket, to further insulate the pit.

UNCOVERING THE PIT

Use the spade to dig and sweep the earth away and, wearing protective gloves, carefully remove the metal sheet and bring the meat out.

To revive an evening bonfire, pull the grate out and throw dry logs into the pit.

Insert a meat thermometer into the center of the joint. This is essential for safety. Firepit cooking is a great deal of fun but is rarely an exact science, so if the temperature reads lower than the minimum temperatures on page 12, put the joint into a low oven to finish cooking through.

Persistence and toil in tending to and building the pit should, reward you with an incredibly tender, smoky supper.

STICKY DATE AND GINGER CAKE

SERVES 8 TO **10**
PREP 20 MINUTES, PLUS 20
  MINUTES SOAKING
COOK ABOUT 1 HOUR

FOR THE CAKE
9 ounces medjool or hadrawi
  dates, pitted and roughly
  chopped
½ cup dark brown sugar
10 tablespoons unsalted butter,
  softened
4 spheres preserved ginger in
  syrup, finely chopped, plus
  syrup from the jar
2 eggs
generous 1¾ cups all-purpose
  flour
1½ teaspoons baking powder
1 rounded teaspoon ground
  ginger
pinch of salt
scant ½ cup pecans, finely
  chopped

FOR THE GINGER-TOFFEE
  SAUCE
1¼ cups heavy cream
1 cup dark brown sugar
pinch of salt
3 tablespoons syrup from the
  preserved ginger jar
pinch of ground ginger

STICKY TOFFEE WITH A KICK OF GINGER, you can't go wrong with this one; it's exactly the kind of dessert that late-fall evenings demand. Just don't skimp on the sauce; it's essential that it soaks right through the cake.

To get the timings to work when making the whole menu, bake this the night before or in the morning. The sponge will have longer to soak up the toffee sauce, and you can tick off the dessert as well as freeing up the oven for the party.

On the subject of adding salt to sweet things, I find a judicious amount balances out sugar, especially in the case of toffee sauces. It's a valuable rule that Southeast Asia has known for many years.

Preheat the oven to 350°F. Line an 8- by 30-inch pan with nonstick parchment paper.

Cover the chopped dates with ⅔ cup boiling water and set aside for 20 minutes.

Beat the sugar and butter together until light with electric beaters or a wooden spoon. Add 3 tablespoons syrup from the preserved ginger jar. Now beat in the eggs, one by one to minimize curdling. Sift the flour, baking powder, and ground ginger over and quickly fold in with the salt, using a metal spoon or spatula. Fold in half the nuts, half the chopped ginger, and all the dates and their liquid. Pour into the pan and bake for 45 minutes until risen and firm to the touch.

Meanwhile, make the sauce. Simmer all the ingredients together, stirring until combined. Set aside to cool slightly.

Pierce the warm cake all over with a skewer and pour about half the syrup on top. Leave for at least an hour, or cover and leave overnight. Warm through in a low oven before serving.

Sprinkle the cake with the remaining nuts and preserved ginger. Serve the remaining syrup alongside, with vanilla or toffee ice cream.

FAMILY-STYLE NEW YEAR'S EVE SUPPER FOR 16

HOMEMADE PASTRAMI | **CURED SALMON** *A board of seeded soda bread, pickles, and mustards* | **LUXURIOUS TART OF BUTTERY LEEKS, MASCARPONE, AND SMOKED GARLIC** | ARUGULA-CELERY ROOT SALAD | **AMARETTI CAKE WITH FIG COMPOTE** | BLACK FOREST SUNDAES

Generously filling a table with handsome and celebratory food, then stepping back, allowing people to serve themselves as they wish, fills my heart with joy. No dishing up, no adorning of multiple plates as if this were a restaurant and not my home, just a relaxed, busy atmosphere, with the odd bit of friendly jostling thrown in.

This is a distinguished, mellow menu, with a couple of seriously impressive recipes to usher in the New Year. Time and planning are the key. Much can be—needs to be—made in advance. The salmon has to be started a few days earlier; the pastrami needs over a week; the cake and compote can be made a couple of days ahead. As can components of the tart and the sundaes. The idea is to get well ahead of the game. If you are making some, or all, of the menu, write lists and sketch a rough timetable, so you know what you're doing and when. I have tried to write the recipes—except the pastrami—so they are easily halved, or doubled, if you have vastly fewer or more guests. The menu will comfortably stretch to feed a couple or so more, so don't turn extras away.

Space is of utmost importance, so beg, borrow, or hire an extra table or three. Don't fret if they're ugly, just throw a tablecloth over the top. Smaller tables could house the sundaes, or stand as a drinks area, to free up some space on the table so it's not too cramped.

Two dessert choices are an indulgence. Though what better time to indulge than on New Year's Eve? You could negotiate this in several ways: choose the one that appeals more (kids, large and small, love a sundae; the cake is probably more suited to the grown-ups), or make just one cake and serve along with the sundaes. Finally, you could serve modest portions of cake as a dessert and the black forest sundaes at midnight.

HOMEMADE PASTRAMI

SERVES 16 (10 IF MAKING LARGE ROUNDS OF SANDWICHES WITH NO OTHER ACCOMPANIMENTS)
PREP 1 HOUR, PLUS COOLING AND SOAKING TIME
CURE 8 DAYS
COOK 3½ TO 4 HOURS, PLUS ½ TO 1 HOUR STANDING

FOR THE CURE

12 ounces rock salt
1 ounce Prague powder no. 1 (see introduction)
¾ cup light brown sugar
1 tablespoon juniper berries, crushed
2 blades of mace
pinch of red pepper flakes
4 bay leaves
1¼-inch piece of fresh gingerroot, sliced
4 allspice berries
2 whole cloves
4 fat garlic cloves, bruised

FOR THE BEEF AND SMOKING

4½-pound bottom round beef
handful of wood chips or chunks, such as apple or cherry, soaked in water for 1 hour

FOR THE DRY RUB

1 tablespoon smoked paprika
2 tablespoons black peppercorns, crushed
2 tablespoons coriander seeds, crushed
2 tablespoons yellow mustard seeds, crushed
2 tablespoons brown sugar
1 tablespoon sea salt
4 garlic cloves, minced

SOME RECIPES LEAVE YOU WITH A KEEN SENSE OF ACHIEVEMENT and this is definitely one of them. Fabulous sandwiches will be yours, and as part of a spread with homemade bread, pickles, salad, and cured salmon? You will be popular.

The minute amount of sodium nitrite found in Prague powder number 1 gives the finished pastrami its characteristic pink color and retards the growth of botulism. It is optional though, and if you can't find it to buy via mail order or online, leave it out.

Start by making the cure. Place all the ingredients in a large pan and add 4 quarts of water. Slowly heat, stirring, until the sugar and salt have utterly dissolved. Turn off the heat and let cool completely; then chill for a few hours.

Trim any tough membrane and sinew from the beef, also thinning any thick plaques of fat. Submerge in the cure, either in a nonreactive pot or bowl, or in a very large, doubled-up, and sealable plastic food bag. The beef should be fully submerged and—in the case of the bag—any air excluded. Leave in the refrigerator for 8 days (2 days per 1 pound 2 ounces), turning every day. Then submerge the joint in plenty of cold water and soak for 1 to 2 hours. Rinse in a colander, drain, and dry thoroughly with paper towels.

At some point during this process, make the dry rub. Combine all the ingredients and use immediately, or keep chilled in a lidded container for up to 3 days, until needed.

When ready to smoke and cook, preheat the oven to 275°F. Spread the rub over the surface of the meat, pressing it in firmly. Some will inevitably fall off, so just scoop it up and pat it on top.

Prepare a makeshift smoker by first sitting a metal rack on the bottom of a large casserole or wok. I use a smallish, circular wire rack. In a pinch, you can use a thick snake of scrunched-up foil instead, but whatever you use has to suspend the joint at least 1½ inches above the base of the cooking pot. Sit the beef on top and fit the lid on, just to check that it fits comfortably. All being well, cut out very large sheets of extra-wide foil. You'll need 10 sheets, stacked on top of each other. Line the wok or casserole with 5 sheets of the stacked foil, leaving all the excess to overhang the pan all the way around. Use the remaining foil sheets to line the inside of the lid in the same way, letting the excess overhang all around.

Drop the soaked wood onto the bottom of the pan, followed by the metal rack. Place the whole lot over medium-high heat. Cover with an askew baking sheet to hold the heat in and, when the wood is hot enough to be really smoking nicely, remove from the heat.

Working quickly, take the lid off and pour ⅔ cup water onto the wood. Lower the beef onto the rack and carefully top the pan with its lid, making sure all the foil is hanging out. Now roll and scrunch all the layers of foil together firmly, sealing the smoking beef in. Slide into the oven and bake for 3½ to 4 hours. I would give a thick, round piece of bottom round beef the whole four hours; a thinner, flatter piece 30 minutes less.

Remove from the oven and let sit, lidded and unwrapped, for 30 minutes to 1 hour before breaking into the foil. The pastrami can be sliced and served immediately, or make it a day or two ahead of time and keep chilled. It is best warm, so wrap in foil and reheat thoroughly in a low oven when needed.

Slice the meat thinly and lay out on a board, with the mustards, pickles, and bread on the table (see page 153). A few chicory leaves and sprigs of dill eaten alongside will add freshness. Eat within a week, or slice and freeze in small freezer bags; it will keep for up to 3 months. Reheat gently (a microwave is good), or wrap in foil and warm through in a low oven to retain the moisture.

CURED SALMON

IF THE PRECEDING PASTRAMI CAN BE POLITELY TERMED "A PROJECT," THIS ONE IS AN ABSOLUTE CINCH. You won't even need to turn the oven on to end up with a stunning side of cured salmon. I can think of no better, or easier, food for a crowd.

To keep the smoky theme alive, marrying the salmon with its costars, pastrami and tart with smoked garlic (see page 150), I have included smoked salt in the recipe below. Though a wonderful and surprisingly subtle ingredient, smoked salt is entirely optional. Please use extra standard rock salt if you cannot find, or have no wish to use, its smoked counterpart.

Pin-bone the salmon, running your fingers up and down the flesh to detect the bones, pulling any out with tweezers. Sit the fish on a couple of sheets of plastic wrap.

Lightly crush the dill or fennel, coriander, and caraway seeds with the peppercorns in a mortar and pestle. Chop half the fennel herb and mix it in, with the brown sugar and salts.

Spread this mixture over the surface of the salmon and wrap it tightly in the plastic wrap. Place in a roasting pan and chill for 3 to 4 days, turning the salmon over when you remember.

Unwrap the now-firm salmon and wipe off as much of the marinade as possible. Holding the fish under the cold faucet, give it a very brief rinse. Dry by dabbing the surface with paper towels.

If you have room in your freezer, you can freeze the whole side for a couple of hours, to make it easier to slice. This isn't strictly necessary, however, and you can just slice the salmon as is. Chop the remaining fennel herb and sprinkle over the salmon. To slice, start at the tail end of the fish and work backward, using a very sharp knife and cutting diagonally down to the skin and sweeping away from you, next to the skin, to free each piece. Make the slices as thin as you like, though I prefer them to be a sturdy ¾–½ inch.

SERVES 16, WITH ACCOMPANIMENTS
PREP 30 MINUTES
CURE 3 TO 4 DAYS

3½ pounds skin-on side of salmon, the freshest you can get
2 tablespoons dill or fennel seeds
2 tablespoons coriander seeds
1 tablespoon caraway seeds
1 tablespoon black peppercorns
handful of fennel herb
1 cup light soft brown sugar
3½ ounces rock salt
1 ounce smoked salt (or an extra 1 ounce rock salt)

LUXURIOUS TART OF BUTTERY LEEKS, MASCARPONE, AND SMOKED GARLIC

MAKES 1 ENORMOUS TART
PREP 50 MINUTES, PLUS AT
    LEAST 1½ HOURS CHILLING
COOK 2 HOURS

FOR THE PIE DOUGH

1 cup (2 sticks) unsalted butter,
    chilled and cubed, plus more
    softened butter for the pan
generous 3⅓ cups all-purpose
    flour, plus more to dust
1 teaspoon salt
1 egg, separated

FOR THE FILLING

pinch of saffron
scant ½ cup light cream
12 large, fat leeks, trimmed, very
    well washed and thickly sliced
4 tablespoons unsalted butter
½ ounce smoked garlic cloves,
    crushed
5 eggs, plus 2 egg yolks
1⅓ cups mascarpone
2¼ ounces Parmesan cheese
bunch of chives, finely snipped

THIS IS A TART WITH SERIOUS HEFT, but it retains a certain elegance. A rustic elegance, perhaps. You will need a lot of pie weights, more than I had in the house, so I used a couple of bags of dried beans that had been hanging around for too long.

Giving a weight quantity for garlic may seem odd, but anyone who has witnessed those monster smoked garlic bulbs will understand the sheer size of each clove. I buy mine online. A note on the pie dough: you could substitute 1-pound 2-ounce bought, all-butter basic pie dough and the world would still turn.

Start with a deep, 10½-inch diameter springform cake pan. Lightly butter the inside of the pan, then dust the butteriness with flour, tapping and turning the pan and tipping out any excess.

Using the pulse button of a food processor, whizz the butter, flour, and salt together for a couple of minutes, until it looks like coarse sand. Tip into a bowl and, using a table knife, cut in the egg yolk and just enough iced water to get the mixture clumping. Tip onto a counter and lightly bring together. Flatten to form a round, wrap in plastic wrap, and chill for at least 1 hour, or up to 3 days.

Remove the dough from the refrigerator about 30 minutes before needed. On a lightly floured counter, roll the dough out to the thickness of ⅛ inch. Line the pan, pushing it up the sides and right into the "corners" with a small ball of dough. Leave a good overhang. Chill for at least 30 minutes, a couple of hours if you have time. Preheat the oven to 375°F.

Scrunch up a large sheet of parchment paper to make it more malleable, then line the dough with it and fill with pie weights, dried beans, or raw rice. Whatever you use, it needs to reach right to the top or the sides could collapse in. Slide onto a baking sheet and bake for 20 minutes, before gingerly removing the paper and beans. Bake for another 5 minutes or so, until the crust looks cooked and "sandy" but is still pale in color. Remove from the oven and immediately brush the pie dough all over with the egg white, to seal and keep it crisp when the filling goes in. Trim the crust flush with the pan. The case will keep, well wrapped, for a couple of days.

Reduce the oven temperature to 325°F. Soak the saffron in the cream. In a large pan with a close-fitting lid, gently soften the leeks

CONTINUED . . .

and a pinch of salt in the butter. The heat should be very low and the lid on very tight for 15 to 20 minutes, until the leeks are very soft but still keeping their shape. Remove the lid, add the garlic, and cook for a couple of minutes more. Set aside to cool.

Whisk the eggs, egg yolks, mascarpone, and saffron-infused cream together. Finely grate half the Parmesan into the custard and add the chives, seasoning generously with pepper. Spoon half the cooked leeks into the pastry shell and—slowly, slowly—pour half the custard over, jiggling the pan every now and then to distribute everything evenly. Repeat with the remaining leeks and custard, finishing by shaving the rest of the Parmesan over the top. Bake for 1 hour 20 minutes, covering loosely with foil if it appears to be browning too much on top. It should be a pale gold.

Let cool in the pan, set on a wire rack, for an hour, before removing the sides. If there is someone with you, get them to help you slide the tart from its bottom to the plate; pry it away with a palette knife or spatula, if needed. Cut into 16 wedges and serve with Arugula–Celery Root Salad (see below).

ARUGULA–CELERY ROOT SALAD

SERVES 16 AS A SIDE SALAD
PREP 20 MINUTES

3-4 lemons, 1 cut into wedges
    and the juice of the rest
1 small celery root
½ cup virgin canola or extra-
    virgin olive oil, or to taste
large pinch of sugar, or
    1 teaspoon honey
7 ounces wild arugula

A SIMPLE, RAW SALAD TO ADD COLOR AND CRUNCH and to soothe the beleaguered cook's brow; you can put this together in a jiffy. The dressing can be made a couple of days ahead and refrigerated if it makes life easier. The celery root can also be pared a few hours ahead; keep it chilled in its bowl of lemon water.

Have ready a bowlful of cold water with four lemon wedges squeezed in, to prevent the cut celery root from browning. Pare the skin from the whole celery root, cutting any root remnants away. Cut into quarters and use either a mandolin or a swivel vegetable peeler to shave long, thin slices from each wedge. As you shave the celery root strips off, drop them into the bowl of lemon water.

Whisk the oil, the juice of two lemons, and the sugar or honey together with a splash of water, seasoning generously with salt and pepper. Add a little more oil or more lemon juice, to taste, as you wish. Just before serving, drain the celery root strips thoroughly, dry out the bowl, and use it to mix your salad. Toss the celery root, arugula, and dressing together and divide between two bowls.

A BOARD OF SEEDED SODA BREAD, PICKLES, AND MUSTARDS

LIGHT HANDS WITH A LIGHT TOUCH produce the best soda bread, so don't overwork or overmix the dough. Now is not the time for kneading. Using all white spelt or all-purpose flour in this recipe makes the resulting bread a little more polite and refined, but you could go in the other direction, as I normally do, and replace some with the same weight of whole grain flour. Replace the seeds with a handful of chopped herbs, if you like. Or try adding a handful of rolled oats and topping the shaped loaves with a sprinkle of them. Generally, I find people to be less sensitive to the gluten in spelt flour, so I tend to use it for large gatherings where the chances of somebody having a slight intolerance (not the same as a full-blown intolerance or allergy!) is higher.

Preheat the oven to 400°F and line a large baking sheet with a piece of nonstick parchment paper.

Measure the flours into a large mixing bowl and stir with a balloon whisk. This is to introduce air and break up any lumps, instead of sifting. Stir in the sugar, baking soda, and salt. Rub in the butter with your fingertips; this will take a while with this amount of flour.

Swapping to a wooden spoon, quickly stir in the buttermilk or yogurt and milk, followed by 4 ounces of the seeds. Mix with a palette knife to form a rough dough, sweeping the flour up from the bottom as you give the bowl a quarter turn. Don't overwork the mixture or it will be tough; it should be just combined. The baking soda will have started its magic, so move quickly as you form the dough into two bonny, round loaves. Sit them on the baking sheet and make a deep cross in the top of each. Gently press the remaining 2¼ ounces seeds (about 2 tablespoons each) over the tops and bake for about 45 minutes, until golden and hollow-sounding when tapped underneath. Cover the loaves with a loose sheet of foil if they are browning too fast. Cool on a wire rack, covered with a dish towel if you would prefer the crusts to soften slightly in their own steam.

To serve, put the loaves on wooden boards, with a bread knife to cut slices (though you could slice them first, if you prefer). Accompany with jars of mustard—whole grain, Dijon, sweet—and bowls of butter, drained cornichons, pickled baby onions, dill sprigs, and fresh chicory leaves.

MAKES 2 LARGE LOAVES
PREP 15 MINUTES
COOK 45 MINUTES

FOR THE BREAD
5 cups white spelt flour or
   all-purpose flour
scant 2¼ cups rye flour
1½ tablespoons superfine sugar
2 teaspoons baking soda
2 teaspoons salt
4½ tablespoons unsalted butter,
   cubed
scant 4¼ cups buttermilk, or 3⅓
   cups lowfat yogurt mixed with
   scant ⅔ cup whole milk
6½ ounces mixed seeds
   (pumpkin, sunflower, sesame,
   hulled linseed, etc.)

TO SERVE
A selection of mustards and
   pickles, butter, fresh dill,
   and chicory leaves

Homemade, infused alcohol is delightful throughout the year, especially when there are plenty of ripe summer berries and pit fruits about. They feel particularly apt around Christmas, when charming cocktails—not to mention presents that won't cost a fortune—are much in demand.

There are so many directions in which you could take each infusion, it really is down to personal taste whether you go with sweet fruit, citrus, herb, fire, or spice, or a combination. Use the ideas below as a guideline and don't forget ripe fruits when at their best: plums, peaches, and nectarines; summer and fall berries in any combination; elderberries, or sweet pineapple (which combines well with black peppercorns). Vodka will carry flavors well without overwhelming them, but you could experiment with other alcohols.

Some, rhubarb for example, will need a little sugar to temper the sharpness, and this should be added to taste. The amounts I have given are merely a guide, skewed toward the lower end of sweet, so taste and slowly add more, until you reach the desired strength.

Start with a 750 ml bottle of vodka, nothing too fancy, but preferably not akin to paint stripper. A middle-of-the-road bottle will do nicely.

You'll also need a large—and scrupulously clean—pickle jar, or similar. It should be big enough to hold the vodka, plus a little extra to account for the added ingredients.

This really couldn't be simpler to prepare; you only need to add your chosen ingredient(s) to the vodka in the pickle jar and leave for as long as directed for each. Keep the jar in a cool, dark place and give it a gentle turn every now and then to redistribute the infusion.

The timings I have given can, of course, be altered as you wish, so taste the vodka while it infuses, stopping the process when you are happy with the strength. Add more of the infusing ingredient or leave for longer, if needed. If you feel the results are too strong, dilute with plain vodka.

Once infused, strain the vodka into a large pitcher, through a fine strainer. Now pour the vodka into sterilized bottles of your choice. Seal or screw on lids and adorn with an identifying label, including the date.

Keep the bottles in a cool, dark place. They'll last for a few months, though the flavors will not be as bright after a time. Those with a roomy freezer should try storing the vodka there; the liquid will thicken to a slightly syrupy consistency.

A FEW IDEAS:

STRAWBERRY

Ideal for those with a sweet drinking tooth; a Barbie-pink and intensely flavored vodka.
Hull and quarter 3½ cups ripe, red strawberries, removing white parts. Leave in the vodka for five days, until the berries have turned white.

RHUBARB

A touch of sugar offsets astringent rhubarb, which should be milder in its pink, winter months. Add more or less sugar depending on taste and time of year. This pale pink spirit makes a beautiful gift.
Chop 1 pound 2 ounces rhubarb and add to the vodka with ½ cup superfine sugar. Infuse for six days.

APRICOT OR PLUM STONES

Both apricot and plum stones add a delicious, almond-like note to vodka, not dissimilar to kirsch.

Crack a handful of apricot or plum stones (I crush them with a heavy mortar) and add to the vodka. Add a little superfine or light brown sugar, if you like. Leave for two weeks, or up to a month.

CUCUMBER

Cool, clean, (dare I say virtuous?) properties.

Slice four large, washed cucumbers into thin rounds. Add to the vodka and leave for four days.

VANILLA

Sweet and beautifully perfumed, in my experience, girls like this one more than the boys.

Split two fat, sticky vanilla beans and add to the vodka. Leave for five days before tasting, then strain or set aside for up to two weeks in total, or until flavored to your liking. Add brown sugar or superfine sugar before or after infusing, if you like.

If you leave this for a month, and add two extra vanilla beans, you will have vanilla extract.

PEAR AND CINNAMON

This makes a great addition to mulled ciders. Replace the pears with apples, if you prefer.

Add three large cinnamon sticks and five sliced, ripe pears to the vodka and let infuse for five days or up to a week. Add sugar, if you like.

LEMON

Lemon is always a success and the resulting alcohol is incredibly versatile; like limoncello without the sugar. Add superfine sugar, to taste, if you like the idea.

Make sure you include only the lemon zest, with no juice or pith. Add the zest of three large, unwaxed lemons to the vodka and leave for a week.

LAVENDER AND ROSEMARY

A fragrant and rather grown-up infusion. I like this with orange juice or soda, a squeeze of lemon, and plenty of ice. Add sugar to taste, if you like.

Bruise two small sprigs of lavender and a sprig of rosemary by crushing them with your fingers to release their fragrant oils. Add to the vodka and leave for three to five days.

CHILI

A fabulous use for homegrown chilies.

Cut slits in your chilies—about six work well but use fewer if they are fire-filled—and add to the vodka. Leave for four days, then taste; leave for a week for more spice.

If your vodka turns out to be rather too hot for your taste, add sugar syrup and lemon juice to cool each serving or cocktail down a notch or two.

GINGER

You might want to temper ginger's fire with sugar or honey. A touch of lemon zest goes very well too.

Peel and chop a fat thumb of fresh ginger root. Add to the vodka with ¼ cup superfine sugar, if you like, and leave for five days, or up to two weeks.

AMARETTI CAKE WITH FIG COMPOTE

**SERVES 8, BUT CAN EASILY BE
DOUBLED**
PREP 40 MINUTES
COOK 1¼ HOURS

FOR THE FIG COMPOTE

3 tablespoons light soft
   brown sugar
3 bay leaves
1 sprig of thyme
12 plump, firm figs, black if
   possible, trimmed and halved,
   plus more to serve
5 tablespoons marsala

FOR EACH CAKE

scant 1 cup superfine sugar
generous 1 cup unsalted butter,
   very soft
5 eggs, at room temperature
scant ¾ cup all-purpose flour
2½ teaspoons baking powder
3½ ounces marzipan, chilled,
   then coarsely grated
¼ teaspoon salt
2¾ cups ground almonds
3 tablespoons yogurt or
   buttermilk
3½ ounces ratafia or crisp
   amaretti cookies, roughly
   crushed

FOR THE AMARETTO SYRUP

¾ cup superfine sugar
1 vanilla bean, split
3 tablespoons amaretto

THERE IS A CHOICE TO MAKE HERE: if a sophisticated cake, studded with ratafia cookies and soaked with amaretto syrup would be a more fitting finish than sundaes, double the recipe and make two, with a double batch of compote. If you feel both desserts would go down well, make one cake and cut it into slivers to serve with the compote, before or with the sundaes. There will be more than enough sugar to go around. Any leftovers keep perfectly for a few days in a cool place; the texture and flavor seem to improve after a day or two.

To make the compote, scatter the brown sugar over the bottom of a large skillet and set over medium heat. When the sugar begins to melt, add the bay leaves, thyme, and figs—in one layer, if possible —cut-sides down. Cook for a couple of minutes, to caramelize the figs, then increase the heat to high and add the marsala, allowing it to bubble fiercely. Turn the figs over carefully and add ⅔ cup water. Simmer briskly until the liquid is slightly syrupy. Let cool, then use immediately, or keep covered and chilled for up to 4 days.

For the cake, preheat the oven to 350°F. Prepare a 9-inch springform cake pan by lining the bottom and sides with nonstick parchment paper.

With the paddle attachment of a food mixer, beat the sugar and butter until pale and light. Add the eggs, one by one, as you beat. If the mixture curdles, add a spoonful of the flour between each egg.

Sift the flour and baking powder over and add the marzipan (separating the strands as much as possible). Fold in with a spatula. Now scatter the salt and almonds over, followed by the yogurt or buttermilk, and fold those in. Last, fold in the ratafia or amaretti.

Scrape into the pan and bake in the center of the oven for 1 hour, until deep gold and firm to the touch. Keep the oven closed for the first 30 minutes but, after that, cover with foil if it browns too fast.

Meanwhile, make the amaretto syrup. Put the sugar in a pan with the vanilla bean and 1¼ cups water. Dissolve the sugar over gentle heat, stirring, then simmer for 8 to 10 minutes, until slightly thickened. Remove from the heat and stir in the amaretto. Let cool.

Pierce the hot cake with a skewer and pour half the syrup over. Let cool in the pan; it is lovely slightly warm. Serve each slice with three fresh fig halves and the compote. Offer the remaining syrup in a pitcher on the side. Crème fraîche is also welcome here.

BLACK FOREST SUNDAES

ONCE ALL THE COMPONENTS HAVE BEEN MADE, chopped, or toasted and set out on a side table with spoons and tall sundae bowls, your guests can form an orderly queue and dive in, constructing the sundae of their wicked dreams. Multiple, small bowls of everything will prevent a scrum and get everybody served quickly.

To get the ice cream ready for easy serving, space scoops out on a couple of baking sheets and open-freeze for up to twenty-four hours (any more and it will turn too frosty on the outside). Either serve from the freezer, to order, or pile the scoops into frozen serving bowls and put out with the other ingredients. All the components are easily halved, to serve a more manageable eight.

WHAT I PUT OUT TO MAKE 16 SUNDAES

2²/3 cups pecans, toasted and chopped

11 ounces dark chocolate, shaved or finely chopped

7 ounces white chocolate, shaved or finely chopped

1³/4 cups crème fraîche, with 2 tablespoons brown sugar marbled through

14-ounce tub vanilla ice cream, in small scoops

14-ounce tub chocolate ice cream, in small scoops

Chantilly Cream (see below)

Chocolate Sauce (see below)

Cherry Compote (see page 160)

Best Brownies (see page 160)

CHANTILLY CREAM

A nostalgically frothy and just-sweet-enough confection; use it as an accompaniment to any number of cakes, tarts, and compotes.

Combine the cream, sugar, and vanilla seeds in a mixing bowl. Whip lightly, until the cream just holds its shape.

SERVES 16, AS PART OF THE SUNDAE SPREAD
PREP 5 MINUTES

1³/4 cups heavy cream

1¹/2 tablespoons confectioners' sugar, sifted

1 vanilla bean, split

CHOCOLATE SAUCE

This sauce begins life with a relatively thin consistency, but it will thicken as it cools, retaining its glossiness. Don't skip the salt; just a touch will balance all that sweetness.

Bring everything but the chocolate to a boil with 2 cups water, turn off the heat, and stir in the chocolate until the sauce becomes smooth and glossy. Put a folded cloth, napkin, or towel beneath and serve the warm sauce from the pan or from a warmed bowl. Heat through gently or blast in a microwave for a few seconds to rewarm halfway, if necessary.

ENOUGH FOR 16 SUNDAES, BUT CAN EASILY BE HALVED
PREP 5 MINUTES
COOK 2 MINUTES

scant 1 cup dark corn syrup

1¹/2 cups unsweetened cocoa

large pinch of sea salt

7 ounces good, dark chocolate, chopped

CONTINUED . . .

CHERRY COMPOTE

IT GOES WITHOUT SAYING THAT YOU CAN make this with pitted, fresh cherries in the summer months, to go with vanilla ice cream.

ENOUGH FOR 16 SUNDAES, BUT CAN EASILY BE HALVED
PREP 5 MINUTES
COOK 5 MINUTES

4 x 14-ounce cans cherries in natural juice
1¼ cups red wine
scant ⅓ cup superfine sugar
3½ tablespoons arrowroot

Drain the cherries thoroughly, reserving their juice. Measure out scant 1¼ cups of juice (if using fresh cherries, just use water instead), and pour into a pan with the fruit, wine, and sugar. Bring everything to a boil and simmer, stirring for a few minutes. Slake the arrowroot in a small dish by stirring in a splash of water to make a loose paste. Add this paste to the pan and simmer for about 1 minute, stirring until thickened. Remove from the heat and let cool slightly before serving in a warmed bowl.

BEST BROWNIES

Line a 9 by 13-inch brownie pan with nonstick parchment paper. Preheat the oven to 375°F. Gently melt 7 ounces good-quality chocolate and scant 1 cup unsalted butter together, stirring until smooth and glossy. Set aside to cool slightly. Beat 4 large eggs, 1 cup superfine sugar, ¾ cup light brown soft sugar, and 1 teaspoon vanilla extract together in the bowl of an electric mixer (or using handheld beaters) for a couple of minutes, to give the finished brownies a velvety texture. Sift in scant 1 cup all-purpose flour (or, for a wheat-free version, sprinkle over 1⅓ cups ground almonds instead), ½ teaspoon baking powder, and scant ¼ cup sifted cocoa. Pour in the melted chocolate and butter mixture with ½ teaspoon sea salt. Beat briefly to combine and stir in another 3½ ounces chopped dark chocolate. Scrape into the prepared pan, reduce the oven temperature to 350°F, and bake for 35 to 40 minutes, until almost firm in the middle. When just warm or cool (leave them to firm up in the pan for at least 30 minutes before you start wielding that knife), turn out carefully, and cut the brownies into 16 bars or 32 small squares. They'll keep in an airtight container for up to 4 days.

COZY WEEKEND AWAY FOR 6

CRISP SAGE LEAVES WITH ANCHOVIES
**HUNTER'S RABBIT STEW AND
PAPPARDELLE** | *Roasted banana shallots,
manchego, and thyme* | **PEARS DIPPED IN HONEY
CARAMEL WITH SOFT CHEESE** | RYE WAFERS

A truly wintry supper of rich, umami notes and golden tones. You won't need too many ingredients or any fancy equipment—always a bonus for a vacation. (And what a relief not to have to rifle through forgotten cupboards in your own house.)

What to take and what to buy in situ presents a dilemma on weekend jaunts; taking half the pantry with you defeats that carefree vacation feeling. In winter, I would suggest traveling with good olive oil, balsamic vinegar, sea salt, and pepper, with a wine or sparkling drink that you love. Don't forget the bottle opener in case there isn't one. It happens.

So that breakfast is taken care of, consider bread that won't spoil—such as sourdough—a package of oats for oatmeal, and dried fruit that, with honey, water, and a cinnamon stick, can be transformed into a warm compote. Unless you're really headed for a remote wilderness, buy most of the fresh items when you get there. With luck, there'll be a good farm shop nearby selling local produce, but do your research first. Lugging a cooler along would be preferable to buying string cheese from the local gas station. With breakfasts and a supper taken care of, if you strike it lucky and the food is good, the local bar or diner can provide sustenance the rest of the time. This is supposed to be a relaxing break.

If you can plan ahead, the rabbit and the rye wafers can be made in advance. But as the weather will be crisp and cold at best, wet and dire at worst, a bit of leisurely kitchen puttering with friends would make for a rather nice afternoon. This gentle prep will pave the way for a predinner sherry with a few sage leaves with anchovy, and onward into supper. As this is a relaxed evening, there is no appetizer. The main course and accompanying shallots will be quite enough. And in lieu of a dessert: a rather stunning cheese course. Choose one magnificent cheese and offer it proudly with the honey-enrobed pears.

CRISP SAGE LEAVES WITH ANCHOVIES

I SERVE THESE WITH PREDINNER DRINKS AND PRETEND TO BE SOPHISTICATED. Honestly, you wouldn't think morsels of salty fish and sage could be this delicious, but they can and they are.

Smoked anchovies in olive oil can be found in suitably swanky delis or online. I couldn't resist. But the standard, unsmoked fillets in oil are just dandy too.

Sandwich a piece of anchovy between two similarly sized sage leaves, pressing down firmly.

Season the flour generously with black pepper and a little salt. Holding the parcels together, dip them in the flour, coating each side lightly; it will stick, as the leaves are slightly furry and the anchovy will have spilt a little oil. Dip them in the egg, shaking off excess, then back into the flour, again shaking off the excess.

Heat enough oil to cover generously the bottom of a large skillet. Add the sage packages—they should sizzle immediately—and fry for a minute on each side, or until golden and crisp. Remove to a plate lined with paper towels to drain briefly. Serve while hot and crisp.

MAKES 18
PREP 10 MINUTES
COOK 5 MINUTES

6 smoked or good-quality
   anchovy fillets in olive oil,
   drained, each cut into 3
36 sage leaves
4 tablespoons all-purpose flour
1 egg, beaten
mild olive oil

Warming winter breakfast ideas

If you prefer a mildly sweet breakfast, this **SIMPLEST BANANA BREAD** only takes a few minutes to mix, and you can tart it up by adding chocolate chips, cocoa nibs, shredded coconut, crushed walnuts or pecans, and/or maple syrup instead of sugar. The addition of coffee—or dark rum if you prefer—brings out the banana flavor magnificently, as does a pinch of ground cinnamon or freshly grated nutmeg.

Use a fork to mash four very ripe, medium-size bananas with 6 tablespoons melted unsalted butter or light olive oil, 2 tablespoons espresso or very strong black coffee, ¾ cup brown sugar, one egg, a pinch of salt, and a few drops of vanilla extract, if you have it, mixing with a wooden spoon. Now quickly fold in 1 teaspoon baking soda and 1½ cups sifted all-purpose flour, plus any extras you might be adding. Pour into a 2¼-pound loaf pan and bake at 350°F for 50 minutes or so, until risen and firm. Cool on a wire rack and serve, sliced into 10 to 12 pieces, plain, or with butter and extra sliced banana.

To start with a regretful negative, broiling **KIPPERS, SARDINES, OR HERRING** will, let's say, "scent," the kitchen and probably the rest of the house. On a more positive note, a buttered and broiled fish is so delicious that I often wonder why they aren't more popular.

Top the fish, skin-side down on a baking sheet, with a few dots of unsalted butter, and slide under a hot broiler until golden and crisp in places. Mashing a little crushed garlic and chopped parsley or chives into the soft butter before broiling is recommended, but may not suit everyone's breakfast-time taste buds. If the smell bothers you, try "jugging" the fish: place them, tails-up, in a very large stockpot, and fill it with just-boiled water. Set aside for 8 to 9 minutes until thoroughly heated through, then drain well. Serve with scrambled eggs, *plenty of black pepper, and a generous wedge of soda bread.*

Ripe and quartered pears, apples, and quinces will make beautiful **ROASTED WINTER FRUITS** when cooked in a low-ish oven the night before; you can reheat them quickly for breakfast. Leave the fruits whole, or halve or quarter if large, and place eight hefty chunks or whole fruits in a roasting pan. Spice every roasting pan of prepared fruits with any combination of whole star anise (just a couple will do), fresh bay leaves, finely grated orange or lemon zest, freshly cracked black pepper, and broken cinnamon bark. Tuck a split vanilla bean in, if the mood strikes you. Add mild honey or sugar to sweeten the fruits—quinces will need far more than pears or apples—and douse the lot in half a wine glass of orange juice or, as Skye Gyngell recommends, verjuice.

To cook, cover loosely with foil and gently bake at 300°F for about 2 hours, gently turning over once or twice, until glazed and very tender. Just apples and/or pears will take less time, but quinces need to soften slowly until orange-pink. If you only have apples and pears, you can speed matters up by roasting the uncovered fruit at 400°F for 20 minutes, stirring a couple of times during cooking. Either way, serve warm, with dollops of Greek yogurt and a generous sprinkling of granola, to make a form of breakfast crumble. This will serve around 8 hungry breakfasters. A glass of freshly squeezed blood orange juice—in season during the winter—would be a delightful accompaniment.

Surely king of the warming breakfast, **oatmeal** doesn't need much explaining, though I do tend to use a mixture of oat bran and whole rolled oats these days. Cooking with a mixture of water and soy milk gives a particularly creamy texture, but just water, or any milk, or a mixture, will all do fine. I always add a pinch of salt.

Baked (for preference) or poached rhubarb compote, gussied up with vanilla or orange zest, and spooned onto each warm bowl of oatmeal, will make a real treat of breakfast for very little effort. Add a few toasted nuts, a little maple syrup, or honey and serve with more hot milk, or even thick cream if you'd like.

This recipe for **BACON SCOTCH PANCAKES** with maple syrup will serve six people, assuming four pancakes per person. If you don't like the idea of bacon in the pancakes, or have vegetarian guests, leave it out, or replace with blackberries or blueberries in season.

Whisk generous 1¾ cups self-rising flour in a mixing bowl, to get some extra air into it and do away with sifting. Add a good pinch of salt and 3 tablespoons superfine sugar. Make a well in the center and gradually whisk in a beaten mixture of four eggs, ¾ cup milk, and 4 tablespoons melted unsalted butter. Incorporate all the flour from the edges as you mix to make a smooth batter, akin to thick heavy cream in consistency. Add a little more milk, if needed.

Broil 18 slices of lean bacon until golden and crisp. Drain on paper towels and break 6 of the slices into 3. Keep the remaining bacon warm.

Place a large skillet or a flat, cast-iron griddle over medium heat. Brush it lightly with paper towels dipped in very soft unsalted butter or a flavorless vegetable oil.

Working in batches, drop tablespoonfuls of batter into the skillet, leaving space for each to spread. Immediately sprinkle each pancake with 3 pieces of bacon and let cook for about 2 minutes, until bubbles break on the surface of the batter and the underside is golden brown. Flip over and cook for another minute or so. Keep the pancakes warm while you cook the remaining batter. Serve in stacks, with the reserved bacon and plenty of maple syrup.

Put the pantry to good use and make **BAKED CHILI**; far more impressive than ready-made versions. The ultimate would be giant Greek gigantes beans, but, outside a Greek deli, they can be hard to find, so use cannellini, haricot, or cranberry instead. Soak scant 3 cups dried beans in plenty of water overnight. Drain, rinse, and cover with fresh water in a large pan. Add a bay leaf and half an onion, bring to a boil, then simmer for 40 minutes, or until almost tender. Beans take varying times to soften, so keep an eye on them.

Preheat the oven to 350°F. Drain the beans and transfer to a roasting pan with generous 1 cup well-flavored vegetable or chicken stock, a chopped red chili or a pinch of dried red pepper flakes, a can of plum tomatoes, two crushed garlic cloves, 2 tablespoons extra-virgin olive oil, a sprig of rosemary, if you have it, and a pinch of sugar. Season well and bake for 45 minutes to 1 hour, until the beans are soft and saucy.

You could also dispense with the soaking and simmering and use two cans of drained beans instead. Add scant ½ cup stock and bake for 30 minutes. Thick toast, made from bread with a bit of character, is a must, but a poached egg or a sausage or two wouldn't go amiss. I once had these with a broiled comte cheese and mushroom sandwich and I must say it was pretty magnificent, as breakfasts go.

HUNTER'S RABBIT STEW
AND PAPPARDELLE

SERVES 6 AS A PASTA SAUCE
PREP 20 MINUTES
COOK 1 HOUR 20 MINUTES

2 ounces smoked bacon cubes

3 tablespoons olive oil

1 large carrot, finely diced

1 large celery stalk, finely diced

1 large onion, finely diced

2 garlic cloves, chopped

1 pound 2 ounces rabbit joints, or 1 large rabbit, skinned and jointed

2 teaspoons juniper berries, crushed

leaves from 1 sprig of rosemary, chopped

generous 1 cup (a large glass) of dry white wine

2 cups good chicken (or rabbit) stock

5 tablespoons heavy cream

1¾ pounds fresh pappardelle pasta, or 1 pound 2 ounces dried pappardelle

manchego or a hard pecorino cheese, finely grated, to serve

ONCE TENDER, THE BRAISED RABBIT IS SHREDDED OR CHOPPED AND RETURNED TO THE PAN to form a rich, but not at all heavy, sauce for fresh pasta. Add cream to taste; 5 tablespoons is really just a guide. It can be replaced with a generous spoonful of mascarpone for an even silkier finish.

In a large casserole, heat the bacon in 1 tablespoon of the oil until they begin to sizzle and brown. Add the vegetables and cook gently, stirring often, for about 8 minutes, or until soft. Stir in the garlic and cook for another 2 minutes, then remove to a large bowl.

Return the empty pan to the heat with another tablespoon of olive oil. Add half the rabbit pieces and cook until browned on all sides. Add to the softened vegetables and repeat with the remaining oil and rabbit pieces. Now return the vegetables and all the browned rabbit to the pan with the juniper, rosemary, wine, and half the stock.

Bring to a boil, cover, and simmer gently for 30 minutes. Remove the rabbit pieces and lay on a board to cool slightly. Shred or dice the meat when cool enough to handle, discarding the bones.

Meanwhile, add the remaining stock to the pan and simmer, uncovered, for 20 minutes or so, until the liquid has reduced by at least two-thirds. When the sauce seems syrupy, return the rabbit to the pan with the cream and heat through for a few minutes. Check the seasoning and adjust to taste, allowing for the salty cheese scattered over each serving. The stew may be made up to 48 hours in advance up to this point and cooled, then chilled. Reheat thoroughly when needed, with an extra splash of water to loosen.

Cook the pappardelle in plenty of boiling, salted water according to the package directions. Drain and immediately toss with the rabbit stew. Serve with plenty of finely grated manchego, as you should have some to hand for the Roast Banana Shallots (see page 170), or pecorino, and eat with the roast shallots.

ROASTED BANANA SHALLOTS, MANCHEGO, AND THYME

NO MORE PEELING ONIONS! A joy for sensitive—and restless —souls. Sweet shallots roast and caramelize slowly with luscious aplomb. I guarantee you'll make these more than once.

Preheat the oven to 325°F.

Slice the shallots in half from top to bottom, trimming any hairy bits from the root as you do so, but leaving them unpeeled. Choose a large ovenproof dish or roasting pan, just big enough to hold the halved shallots in a single layer. Drizzle the bottom with half the olive oil and scatter with two sprigs of thyme. Season with salt and pepper. Tuck the shallot halves in snugly, cut-sides down.

Roast for 50 minutes to 1 hour, or until soft. Increase the oven temperature to 350°F.

Use a spatula to carefully flip the shallots over, so that they all lie with cut-sides upward. Drizzle with the remaining olive oil; add the balsamic vinegar and two more sprigs of thyme. Return to the oven for about 15 minutes, until well caramelized. Scatter with the leaves of the remaining thyme and shave the manchego over with a vegetable peeler. Serve from the dish, with the Hunter's Rabbit Stew and Pappardelle (see page 168).

SERVES 6 AS A SIDE DISH
PREP 15 MINUTES
COOK 1 HOUR

9 banana shallots
4 tablespoons extra-virgin
   olive oil
6 sprigs of thyme
2 tablespoons balsamic vinegar
2 ounces manchego cheese

RYE WAFERS

MAKING YOUR OWN CRACKERS IS A REWARDING, THOUGH COMPLETELY OPTIONAL, PIECE. The seeds can be kneaded into the dough rather than scattered over if you'd rather incorporate them thoroughly, and do use any single variety or combination that appeals. Finely grated Parmesan, dried or finely chopped fresh herbs, red pepper flakes, celery salt, citrus zests, paprika, finely chopped olives, or sundried tomatoes, caraway, cumin, or coriander seeds will all enhance the basic mixture.

Preheat the oven to 425°F, and oil or line three baking sheets.

Preferably in the bowl of a mixer fitted with a paddle attachment (a wooden spoon will also do perfectly well), combine the flours and salt, turn the machine on low, and slowly add the oil and scant ¼ cup of barely warm water. Stop adding water when everything comes together to form a pliable, but not sticky, dough. You may need another spoon or so of water, you may not. This really isn't a temperamental mix at all, so slowly add a little more flour or water as needed to reach the right consistency.

Knead for about 10 minutes, either by hand on a counter, or with the dough hook attachment of a food processor. Cover the bowl with a damp cloth and let rest for 30 minutes or so.

You can use a pasta machine for this next stage but, to be honest, I find it rather fussy and prefer to use a rolling pin. On a floured surface, roll the dough out, one-third at a time. An even thickness of about ⅛ inch is what you're after.

Cut into cracker-sized triangles or squares. You can leave them in elegantly long strips and break them into shards after cooking. Or stamp out circles or more ambitious shapes, if you wish.

Space each batch of wafers out on a large baking sheet and brush lightly with oil. Scatter with one-third of the seeds—inevitably a few will fall off—no matter, bake them anyway and scatter the seeds over the wafers as you serve them. Bake for 8 to 12 minutes, depending on size and thickness, until crisp and curling up prettily at the edges. I find they cool perfectly well on the baking sheets. Repeat to use up all the dough and seeds. Store in an airtight tin for up to 10 days.

MAKES 20 TO 40 CRACKERS, DEPENDING ON SIZE
PREP 25 MINUTES, PLUS ABOUT 30 MINUTES RESTING TIME
COOK 8 TO 12 MINUTES

4 tablespoons extra-virgin olive oil, plus more to brush
¾ cup rye flour, plus more to dust
generous ⅓ cup spelt, or whole grain, or white all-purpose flour
½ teaspoon sea salt
3 ounces mixed seeds (poppy, linseed, sesame, pumpkin, or sunflower, for example)

PEARS DIPPED IN HONEY CARAMEL
WITH SOFT CHEESE

THESE PEARS, ENROBED IN SULTRY CLOAKS OF CRISP CARAMEL, are almost impossibly delightful. A light, mousse-like goat milk cheese is what I offer alongside here, but a salty blue or a molten brie would be equally apt; something to hold up to the dark caramel and fruit. Simply choose a single, signature cheese you love. About 14 ounces to 1 pound 2 ounces will do very well for six after such a hearty main course. If, at other times of the year, plump black or green figs are what you have instead of pears, carefully enrobe the whole fruits with honey caramel. They will be equally as stunning.

Cut a thin sliver from the base of each pear so that it will sit upright, then—and this is the important part—stick the tines of a fork firmly into the base of each so that you can pick it up like a pear lollipop. Lay out in a row.

In a large, heavy-bottomed pan (large to contain the caramel safely, heavy-bottomed to melt the sugar evenly), heat the sugar, honey, salt, and scant ½ cup water together very gently, stirring with a wooden spoon until the sugar has dissolved. Put the spoon aside and increase the heat to get the mixture bubbling steadily. After about 5 minutes, the caramel should darken in color and appear thicker. You are after a deep chestnut hue. At around 300°F on a sugar thermometer, if you're measuring, turn off the heat and immediately take a pear in each hand, holding them by the fork. On NO account should you touch the hot caramel; it will burn severely.

Dip and swirl the pears into the caramel to coat most of the top of each fruit, turning them in the air for at least 10 seconds until set just enough to remove the forks. To do this, gingerly hold the caramel-free base and sit the pears upright. Repeat with the remaining four pears. Serve within 3 or 4 hours, so that the caramel coating remains crisp, accompanied by homemade Rye Wafers (see page 171) or bought crackers and cheese.

SERVES 6
PREP 20 MINUTES
COOK ABOUT 15 MINUTES

6 plump, ripe pears
¾ cup light brown soft sugar
generous ¼ cup thin honey
pinch of salt

MEZZE NIGHT for 12

HONEY-ROASTED BEET AND CARROT SALAD | **STUFFED GRAPE LEAVES (DOLMADES)** | *Golden cauliflower with sesame dressing* | **BRAISED CALAMARI** | CHICKEN OR VEGETABLE KDRA WITH ALMONDS AND COUSCOUS | **BLOOD ORANGE ICE CREAM** | BOUGATSA **FRESH MINT TEA**

This menu should start with a disclaimer: it is in no way authentic. I have magpied from here and there, borrowing influences from Morocco, Greece, Italy, and my notebooks to end up with a handful of easy little dishes that complement each other. The idea is that producing a colorful spread of small plates, along with a majestic kdra (a kind of tagine) and a stunning dessert, won't prove too arduous if you plan the workload over a few days.

Of course, you can cut down and simplify: use a store-bought mayonnaise to accompany the squid; buy your dolmades from a deli (they are usually very good); forget about the bougatsa entirely—it's an extra anyway—or replace it with little squares of store-bought baklava to go with mint tea . . . I could go on, but suggesting you buy everything is rather missing the point of a cookbook!

These mezze recipes will serve twelve as a feast if all are made, but are appetizer-sized for six if you only do a couple. I throw big pillows on the floor to sit on and lay everything out in the middle, or on a low table, with a stack of serving plates and plenty of napkins. Serve the mezze in little dishes and add sliced flatbreads and hummus, if you need to offer more filling fare. It should be easy to create a feeling of plenty.

The kdra will serve six as a main course, more with extra dishes. The ice cream will serve twelve as a stand-alone dessert. The bougatsa pastries are intended to be sliced or at least halved if served with the ice cream, so the recipe makes six; however, if serving them on their own, plan on one whole pastry per person.

MEZZE
HONEY-ROASTED BEET AND CARROT SALAD

IF YOU CAN FIND MULTICOLORED CARROTS AND BEETS at a farmers' market or similar, this vibrant salad is a perfect way to celebrate them; the slow roasting concentrates their natural sugars. By all means, use pretty baby carrots and beets if they have a good flavor—those tiny ones so often don't, though.

Use only as much harissa as you and your guests would like; caution is sensible as too much fire will kill the sweetness of the honeyed vegetables.

Preheat the oven to 350°F. Cut the beets into chunks or wedges a little smaller than the carrot slices; this is not a delicate affair so they don't want to be neatly cubed, just even in size. Toss with the carrots, 1 tablespoon of harissa to start, the honey, olive oil, and plenty of salt and pepper. Spread out on a baking sheet and roast slowly for about 1 hour, stirring occasionally, until the vegetables are caramelized and a little shriveled.

Remove from the oven and squeeze the lemon juice over, tasting gingerly and adding more olive oil, harissa, or honey as you think right. Let cool a little, then stir the cilantro leaves through and serve warm or at room temperature.

SERVES 12 AS PART OF A MEZZE SPREAD
PREP 20 MINUTES
COOK 1 HOUR

1 pound 2 ounces smallish beets, scrubbed and trimmed
1 pound 2 ounces carrots, scrubbed and thickly sliced
1–2 tablespoons good-quality harissa paste, to taste
2 tablespoons light, thin honey, or to taste
2 tablespoons olive oil, plus more to dress
squeeze of lemon juice
small handful of cilantro leaves, roughly chopped

MEZZE
STUFFED GRAPE LEAVES
(DOLMADES)

MAKES ABOUT 26
PREP 30 MINUTES, PLUS
    COOLING AND OPTIONAL
    CHILLING TIME
COOK 1½ HOURS

at least 35 large grape leaves,
    fresh or brined
¾ cup brown long-grain rice
1 large onion, minced
about 4 tablespoons extra-virgin
    olive oil
generous ⅓ cup pine nuts
2 garlic cloves, crushed
⅓ cup golden raisins
handful of mint leaves, minced
handful of dill fronds, minced
finely grated zest and juice of
    1 unwaxed lemon

MAKE THESE A COUPLE OF DAYS BEFORE AND KEEP IN THE REFRIGERATOR, returning them to room temperature about an hour before serving. Their flavors will improve and mellow, and so should you, for there'll be no need to do any last-minute grape leaf stuffing. Ideally, you or a neighbor might have a prolific grape vine to plunder for fresh leaves but, if you get stuck, use blanched cabbage leaves instead. I have gone for a vegetarian filling but do add ground lamb, pork, or beef if you wish, browning it at the beginning with the onion. Any extra dill fronds can be packed into the baking dish with the dolmades to add further fragrance. I like the nuttiness of brown rice, but you can just as well use white.

Place the (drained) grape leaves in a large, heatproof bowl and cover with just-boiled water. Set aside to soak for 15 minutes or so. Meanwhile, rinse the rice well and tip into a pan. Cover with enough water to reach the first knuckle of your upside-down index finger when you rest the tip on the rice. Throw in a pinch of salt, cover with an askew lid, and simmer gently for 20 minutes, or until just tender. If any water remains, drain it off and set the rice aside.

Slowly soften the onion in half the oil, stirring, until translucent. Add the pine nuts and ramp the heat up a little, cooking until both nuts and onions turn pale gold. Remove from the heat and stir in the cooked rice, garlic, raisins, mint, dill, lemon zest, and half the juice. Season with salt and freshly ground black pepper. Preheat the oven to 350°F.

Drain the grape leaves and pick out your best beauties; you want them large and untorn. Use any raggedy leaves to line the bottom of a rectangular baking dish. Lay a first-class leaf on a cutting board, veiny side up (shiny side down) and cut out the coarse part of the stalk. Don't go too mad, leave the leaf as intact as possible. Place a scant tablespoon of filling on the base of the leaf, fold in both sides, and roll away from you firmly to create a neatly plump cigar. It gets easier with practice. Pack the dolmades into the dish, seams down and as tightly as possible to prevent them unrolling. Repeat until you run out of filling or leaves. Pour enough boiling water over to just cover, add the remaining lemon juice and oil, and cover with more raggedy leaves, if you have them. Cover the lot tightly with foil.

Bake for 1 hour, then remove from the oven and weigh down with a couple of cans on top of the foil. Let cool completely. Chill for up to 3 days before serving at room temperature.

MEZZE
GOLDEN CAULIFLOWER
WITH SESAME DRESSING

IF YOU HAVEN'T TRIED ROASTING CAULIFLOWER, DO;
it's so different than the soggy, sad boiled version you may have
suffered through.

The sesame dressing can be made up to a week in advance and kept
chilled. Bring it back to room temperature and thin it with water
when you need it. The sesame seeds themselves have a mind of their
own, so it's safer to toast them separately in a dry skillet, shaking
often, until they are evenly golden, and sprinkling over the cooked
cauliflower to finish.

Pour the sesame seeds into a dry skillet, place over medium heat,
and toast, stirring, until golden and fragrant. Remove from the
skillet and set aside. Preheat the oven to 400°F. Toss the cauliflower
with the oil, cumin, red pepper flakes, and a generous grinding of
salt and pepper. Spread out on a baking sheet and roast for about
25 minutes, shaking occasionally to redistribute, until charred at the
edges. Remove from the oven and scatter with the sesame seeds.

To make the dressing, whisk together all the ingredients with
5 tablespoons water until smooth. Season with salt and pepper
and adjust the lemon juice and honey as needed until it tastes
good to you.

Serve the hot cauliflower with a bowl of the dressing to spoon over.

**SERVES 12 AS PART OF A
  MEZZE SPREAD**
PREP 15 MINUTES
COOK 25 MINUTES

FOR THE CAULIFLOWER
3 tablespoons sesame seeds
1 large cauliflower, cut into
  small florets
4 tablespoons olive oil
1 tablespoon cumin seeds
½ teaspoon dried red pepper
  flakes

FOR THE SESAME DRESSING
4 tablespoons light tahini
  (sesame seed paste)
juice of 1 lemon, or to taste
1 teaspoon honey, or to taste
1 garlic clove, crushed
2 tablespoons extra-virgin
  olive oil

MEZZE
BRAISED CALAMARI
IN TOMATO SAUCE

**SERVES 12 AS PART OF A
MEZZE SPREAD**
PREP 20 MINUTES
COOK 50 MINUTES

FOR THE CALAMARI

4 garlic cloves, finely sliced

2 red chilies, slit lengthwise

3 tablespoons extra-virgin olive
  oil, plus more to serve

3 cups passata (strained
  tomatoes) or canned chopped
  tomatoes

2¼ pounds small squid or
  cuttlefish, cleaned, bodies
  sliced into rings

handful of parsley, roughly
  chopped

FOR THE SAFFRON
MAYONNAISE

pinch of saffron threads

2 egg yolks

1 garlic clove, crushed

1¼ cups very mild olive oil or
  peanut oil

lemon juice, to taste

LONG AND SLOW OR SHORT AND BRISK ARE THE ONLY OPTIONS WHEN COOKING SQUID (kalamari or calamari if you're Greek or Italian. It's a better word than *squid*, don't you think?). Done right, both result in tender, nonrubber band-like flesh. A gentle simmer, as here, with a bounty of garlic and a background note of chili, renders sliced squid absolutely tender, and comforting with very little actual work involved. (I have also had great success with octopus in this recipe.)

To make it simpler still, you could easily buy a lovely, fresh mayonnaise and stir in steeped saffron threads and a little crushed garlic to save yourself a bit of fuss.

Gently heat the garlic, whole slit chilies, and oil together in a large pan, stirring for 2 to 3 minutes as the garlic becomes fragrant but not allowing it to brown. Add the tomatoes and squid rings and tentacles with about ¾ cup water.

Cover with a lid and simmer very slowly for about 45 minutes, until the squid is completely tender. Stir every now and then to check the mixture is not burning on the bottom. If too much liquid remains (the sauce should be thick and rich), remove the lid for the last few minutes of cooking; if the sauce is sticking, add a little extra water. Season to taste with salt and pepper and remove the whole chilies; at this point the calamari can be cooled and chilled for up to 2 days. Reheat gently before serving.

Make the mayonnaise while the seafood simmers. Set the saffron and 1 tablespoon boiling water aside in a little bowl to steep. Use a food mixer or an electric hand whisk and a bowl to beat the egg yolks and garlic together with a pinch of salt. Gradually add the oil (we're talking drop-by-drop at first) as you blend or whisk, increasing to a steady, thin trickle and continuing until all the oil has amalgamated into a thick, glossy mixture. Stir in the saffron and its water, seasoning with a squeeze of lemon and more salt, if needed. Chill for up to 2 days before using.

Finish the hot squid with plenty of chopped parsley and a slick of good extra-virgin olive oil. Serve alongside the saffron mayonnaise.

Introducing games at a party first warrants gauging your potential players. Self-proclaimed hipsters or sneery types will find the very idea tedious in the extreme, but I'd wager that even the naysayers would enjoy themselves, albeit grudgingly, if they ventured into parlor game territory. A drink or two for the adults helps enthusiasm levels greatly. Try to keep the feel lighthearted and the momentum swift, both to avoid boredom or fighting and to prevent any forays into cheesy, Brady Bunch territory.

CEREAL BOX

Bring out this game once any post-dinner slump has passed. It's a simple concept, but one that fells overly ambitious males particularly well (unless your male friends happen to be dancers, yoga teachers, or gymnasts).

This game works best with six to ten players; too many more and matters can become long-winded. Sort your group into two even-ish teams if you like, or play as individuals.

Tear the top flaps from an empty cardboard cereal box. Stand the box in the center of the room. Make sure there's a bit of space available for flailing and falling.

In order, each player approaches the box and attempts to pick it up. The twist is that only feet are allowed to touch the floor and only mouths can be used to lift the box. Any hand, elbow, knee, or other body part touching the floor (or box) will result in immediate elimination, so be prepared to bend and fold your body, as needed.

Once everybody has completed—or been eliminated from—round one, about 1-inch must be torn or cut from the top of the cereal box, shortening it slightly. The game continues as before, knocking out players who falter, fall, or cheat as the rounds go by.

When the box is very low, only the most flexible remain in play and methods of getting low to the ground (usually involving the splits) can get very amusing. The winner is the last man in legal play.

REVEREND CRAWLEY'S GAME

You'll need at least eight players for this one and a spacious room. It's particularly suited to family gatherings, as you might prefer to know your fellow players well.

Get everybody to stand in a circle and link hands, but not with the person to their immediate left or right. Also, each hand must link to a different person. It will take a minute or two to figure out.

You will be left with a big, spaghetti-style muddle of limbs in the middle of the circle. Now you must untie the knot, without unlinking hands. This will involve twisting, crawling through gaps and climbing over arms, until a perfect circle is restored. Occasionally, the outcome will be two separate rings, but it is always surprising.

Famous

Get all the players to write the names of ten well-known people (alive or dead, real or fictional) on individual scraps of paper. Fold or scrunch the papers up and toss them into a hat or bowl. Working in teams, start the clock as one team member picks out a name (without showing it to anybody) and attempts to describe it to the rest of his or her team (without saying the actual name). Each correct name shouted out by the team represents a point. The designated team member should keep picking out and describing names as fast as they can for one minute. When the time is up, quickly move onto the next team.

Play until all the scraps of paper have gone, then tally up the scores. Vary this using charades, or by drawing pictures, instead of verbal descriptions.

MAIN COURSE
CHICKEN KDRA WITH ALMONDS

**SERVES 12 WITH THE MEZZE,
OR 6 AS A MAIN COURSE**
PREP 20 MINUTES
COOK ABOUT 1 HOUR

2 teaspoons ground ginger

large pinch of saffron threads

6 tablespoons unsalted butter,
softened

4 garlic cloves, crushed

small handful of chopped parsley,
plus more to serve

small handful of chopped
cilantro, plus more to serve

12 chicken pieces, skin-on legs
and thighs

1 tablespoon olive oil

2 large onions, finely sliced

2 large cinnamon sticks

4 cups good chicken stock

2 preserved lemons, quartered

3 cups cooked chickpeas (or
2 x 14-ounce cans)

handful of large green olives,
drained and left whole

2/3 cup whole blanched almonds

squeeze of lemon juice

THIS IS ESSENTIALLY A LIGHT AND FRAGRANT CHICKEN TAGINE FROM MOROCCO. I have included a vegetarian variation, along with a mouth-watering couscous.

Mix the ginger and saffron into the butter with the garlic, parsley, cilantro, and plenty of salt and pepper. Dab the chicken dry with paper towels and spread with butter. Sit the chicken snugly in a large tagine or sturdy pan, big enough to hold them in one layer, and place over medium heat. Sprinkle with oil and cook, undisturbed, until golden underneath. Turn and fry until golden all over.

Throw in the onions, cinnamon, and stock and bring to a gentle simmer. Cover and cook over low heat for 20 minutes. Cut out and discard the flesh of the preserved lemons, then slice the zest into thin sticks. Add to the chicken with the chickpeas, olives, and almonds and simmer for another 20 minutes. Taste and stir in the lemon juice; the chicken should be very tender. Scatter with the remaining herbs and serve in its tagine or a large dish.

VEGETABLE KDRA
This serves 6 as main course or 10 as part of a mezze spread. Replace the chicken with 2¾ pounds scrubbed root vegetables, cut into chunks. Use something with integrity and staying power: carrots, parsnips, rutabaga, peeled and halved shallots, pumpkin, squash, and thickly sliced peppers are all ideal. Fry the vegetables and sliced onion in the spiced garlic butter and oil for a few minutes as in the main recipe, then add all the remaining ingredients, reducing the amount of stock to 3⅓ cups, cover, and simmer for 20 minutes, until the vegetables are tender but still holding their shape.

COUSCOUS
If you're not steaming couscous the traditional way (and I'm assuming you won't), it needs plenty of herbs and zest. To make enough for a side dish for 12 as part of a mezze, or 6 to accompany a main course, place 2⅓ cups couscous in a large bowl. Mix in the finely grated zest of an unwaxed lemon, a pinch of saffron, a crushed garlic clove, a little salt and pepper, and a generous helping of cubed unsalted butter. Cover by a scant ½ inch with boiling, full-flavored chicken or vegetable stock, top with a plate, and set aside for 5 to 10 minutes, until the liquid has been absorbed. Season with lemon juice, more salt and pepper, and two handfuls of minced mixed herbs (mint, parsley, cilantro, basil, fennel or dill, tarragon, or chervil). Fluff up with a fork, adding a lug of extra-virgin olive oil.

DESSERT
BLOOD ORANGE ICE CREAM

THIS IS A PALE-HUED ICE CREAM, not the deep garnet you might expect from darker blood oranges. Its taste is superlative—honestly, I can't encourage you enough to make this. The idea of reducing the orange juice down in order to concentrate it is gratefully borrowed from a Martha Stewart recipe.

An ice-cream machine is an investment, so if you can't justify buying one, freeze the ice-cream base in an open container that has a lid, whisking vigorously every hour or so to break up the ice crystals. It will take at least four hours to get very thick, at which point you can put the lid on and freeze until it is scoopable.

To fully celebrate the blood orange, serve with more of the fresh fruit, first slicing the pith and zest away, then slicing into rounds. You can pile the orange slices into a large bowl and serve alongside the ice cream for everyone to help themselves.

You should have about 1 cup of orange juice from the 8 oranges, a little bit extra won't make much difference. Boil the orange juice down in a large pan, simmering it gently, until reduced in volume by two-thirds. Set aside to cool.

Mix the zest with the milk in a separate pan and slowly bring up to boiling point, removing from the heat as the surface begins to steam and shimmer. Set aside for 30 minutes, or longer if you have time.

Return the milk to low heat to warm through. Whisk the egg yolks, sugar, and salt together in a heatproof bowl until pale and airy; the whisk—I'd use an electric one here—should leave a ribbon-like trail when lifted out. Slowly pour the steaming milk onto the egg mixture, whisking all the while. Pour into the cleaned-out pan and return to very low heat, stirring, until the custard thickens enough to coat the back of a spoon. This will take 10 to 15 minutes; be patient, because scrambled eggs won't make a stunning ice cream.

Strain through a strainer into a bowl nestling in a large bowl of ice and stir in the cream. Add the reduced orange juice. If the mixture is not cool, let cool, stirring now and then. Chill well, then pour into an ice-cream machine and churn according to the manufacturer's directions. You may need to do this in two batches. When thick, but not solid, scrape into a lidded container and freeze for at least 4 hours or overnight. The ice cream can be spooned straight from the machine, just let it become a little more firmly set first. Serve with sliced blood oranges (see introduction) and slivered pistachios.

MAKES ABOUT 5 CUPS
PREP 20 MINUTES, PLUS AT LEAST 4 HOURS FREEZING
COOK ABOUT 15 MINUTES, PLUS 30 MINUTES INFUSING

8 blood oranges: finely grated zest of 2; juice of all 8, plus more to serve
2½ cups whole milk
6 egg yolks
generous 1 cup superfine sugar
pinch of sea salt
scant 1¼ cups heavy cream
slivered pistachios, to serve

DESSERT
BOUGATSA

THESE DELIGHTFUL GREEK CUSTARD PASTRIES, crisp and buttery and perfumed with orange flowers and vanilla, are pure indulgence. Halve or slice thickly though, as one each will be far too much after so much food. Serve them with Fresh Mint Tea (see right) and coffee, or paired with Blood Orange Ice Cream (see page 184). They also make a lovely brunch pastry, or a dessert in their own right, in which case make one per person, with poached apricots or berries and sliced peaches in the summer.

MAKES 6
PREP 40 MINUTES, PLUS
    COOLING TIME
COOK ABOUT 35 MINUTES

scant 1½ cups whole milk
pinch of sea salt
1 vanilla bean, split lengthwise,
    seeds scraped out
1 egg and 1 egg yolk, beaten
¼ cup superfine sugar
generous ⅓ cup fine semolina
7 tablespoons unsalted butter,
    plus more for the baking sheet
1 teaspoon orange flower water
    (optional)
finely grated zest of 1 unwaxed
    lemon and 2 teaspoons of its
    juice
12 small or 6 large sheets of
    phyllo pastry dough
ground cinnamon and
    confectioners' sugar, to dust

Heat the milk and salt in a large pan with the vanilla bean and seeds. Bring up to simmering point—the surface will be shimmering—then remove from the heat. Whisk the egg, yolk, and superfine sugar together in a bowl until thick and pale. Remove the vanilla bean from the milk and pour the milk onto the egg mix as you whisk.

Return to the cleaned-out pan over low heat and cook, stirring constantly, for 5 minutes. Sprinkle in the semolina and increase the heat slightly. Keep stirring until the mixture thickens; it will take at least 5 minutes.

Cut 2 tablespoons of the butter into small cubes and stir into the semolina custard. Remove from the heat and keep stirring until the butter has disappeared. Add the orange flower water, lemon zest, and juice. Cover the surface with plastic wrap to prevent a skin forming and set aside to cool completely, the custard will thicken further as it cools.

Preheat the oven to 375°F. Have a large baking sheet, buttered or lined with nonstick parchment paper, ready. Melt the remaining butter and set aside.

If your phyllo is in large sheets, cut them in half horizontally before covering with a damp dish towel to prevent them drying out. You should have 12 small sheets. Working one at a time, brush one side lightly with melted butter, lay another piece on top, and brush with more butter. With the short side near you, spoon a scant 3 tablespoons of cooled custard onto the lower third of the rectangle, spreading it out to form a smaller rectangle of about 3¼ by 2½ inches. Fold the right and left sides in to meet in the middle, then

fold the bottom edge up and fold and roll the phyllo away from you to enclose the custard completely. Seal the edge with melted butter and brush the outside with more butter. Place on the baking sheet and repeat to make 6 pastries.

Bake for about 20 minutes, until golden and crisp. Serve warm or at room temperature. Though best made on the day, they can be made a couple of days in advance and will still be delicious. If making ahead of time, you'll find that the pastry loses its crispness upon sitting and needs a quick blast in the oven to revive it. The filling can be made 3 days in advance and kept chilled.

Combine a little ground cinnamon with confectioners' sugar (about 1 teaspoon of cinnamon to 3 tablespoons sugar, say) and dust over the cooked pastries before serving.

FRESH MINT TEA

Divide fresh mint leaves between little glasses or cups. Be generous. Cover with boiling water and let steep for a couple of minutes. Sweeten with honey for those who want it and stir in a little lemon juice to brighten.

A few more quick ideas and hints for laid-back and hearty ways to feed the hungry hoards.

To make a **SUBLIME ASIAN BEEF SHIN BRAISE** with soy, star anise, and ginger for 10 hungry souls, you will need the following: 4½-pound beef shin on the bone; 1 teaspoon lightly crushed Sichuan peppercorns; peanut oil; ¾ cup light brown sugar (I know, bear with me); 2 thumb-size pieces of fresh gingerroot, peeled and sliced into coins; 5 garlic cloves, sliced; ¾ cup Shaoxing rice wine; 3 whole star anise; the pared zest and juice of 1 large orange; 1 teaspoon salt; 1¼ cups light soy sauce. First generously salt the beef and coat with the crushed Sichuan peppercorns. Use a little peanut oil to sear the shin pieces, in batches, in a large skillet. Set aside in a bowl.

Throw the lot, including the beef and its juices, into a very large, lidded casserole or stockpot and add enough cold water to cover generously. Bring up to a gentle simmer. Skim off any impurities, then slide into a 350°F and forget about it for 4 hours, or until the beef is extremely tender. Ideally, make this the day before and let cool. Skim off the fat and discard the bones. Keep some of the stock back to use in Asian soups and future braises; it freezes well. There should be enough liquid left in the pan liberally to coat the beef shin. Taste and season with more salt or soy sauce, if needed. Reheat thoroughly on the stove and eat with simply steamed pak choi and rice, adorning each plate or bowlful with shredded scallion. Follow with fresh mango, litchis, and ice cream.

This is one I made for 25 of us on Bonfire Night last year and it seemed to go down well. To make **SAUSAGES FOR A CROWD WITH ONION JAM** in warmed baguettes, work on needing three good-quality sausages per person, assuming your friends are as, um, "enthusiastic" as mine. Don't forget the vegetarians. Roast sausages in large roasting pans, spaced well apart and turning at least once, so that they brown evenly. They'll need about 30 minutes at 375°F, depending on thickness. You can coat them with a little honey and whole grain mustard halfway through, if you like.

Warm through some fresh baguettes. Each loaf should be sliced into five, split open, and lightly buttered. Spread a tablespoon of Red Onion Relish with Port (see page 91) inside each and stuff with three, or maybe two, sausages and a few arugula leaves. Hand out with paper napkins.

Failing the onion jam, sliced and fried onions, or a good store-bought chutney or ketchup will do nicely.

It's neither desirable nor practical always to make separate options for vegetarians and meat eaters. Most of us could do with concentrating on vegetables a little more, and this is **A VERY GOOD SOUP FOR A COLD DAY** indeed. Make it as needed, or a day or so before, ready to reheat.

This makes enough for 10, as a main course or a lunch with bread, and perhaps some cheddar or goat cheese.

Roast 2 sizeable, peeled, seeded, and cubed squashes. I had great success with coquina squash recently—it has very dense flesh, similar in looks and taste to a butternut, but sweeter—homegrown butternuts would also be ideal. Toss the cubed squash with olive oil, salt, pepper, and a few rosemary leaves. Roast in a hot oven until caramelized and soft. Meanwhile, slowly soften a couple of large, chopped onions in olive oil in a stockpot; don't rush the onions, allow them time to mellow and gild. Add the squash, a can of plum tomatoes, a sprig of rosemary, and enough vegetable stock to cover generously. Simmer for about 20 minutes, then remove the rosemary and attack the soup with an immersion blender, until smooth. I like this thick, but let it down with extra water until it has a consistency you like. Adjust the seasoning and reheat thoroughly before serving. To go with said soup: A simple soup is indeed a beautiful thing, but if you feel it needs something more, consider making a simple bread dough, such as the base for Herb Fougasse and Fig and Mozzarella Pizzas (see page 34), and turning it into a **STROMBOLI**. After its first rise, punch down the basic bread dough and divide into two circles. Roll and stretch each ball to form a large rectangle (about 6 by 10 inches). Lay out your choice of prosciutto, basil, rosemary or thyme leaves, pesto, tapenade, roasted peppers, pitted olives, capers, torn mozzarella, shaved Parmesan, sunblush or roast tomatoes, and so on in any seasonal combination you like. Roll the dough up from a long edge to form a fat sausage, making sure the seam is underneath to prevent it from bursting open in the oven. Let both loaves to rise on oiled baking sheets, in a warm place and covered with damp dish towels, for about 20 minutes.

Bake at 400°F, for 35 minutes or so, until golden and well-risen. Cool slightly on wire racks and slice thickly to serve with soup in lieu of bread and cheese. The baked loaves freeze perfectly and can be thawed in the refrigerator overnight and reheated.

Throw together an enormous, warm and wintry (and vegetarian) main course **SALAD OF STICKY ROASTED CARROTS, PARSNIPS, AND SHALLOTS** folded with simmered farro, barley, or spelt with lots of toasted pecans, crumbled goat cheese, cooked chestnuts, and chopped parsley. Dress with sherry vinegar, a touch of honey, a scrape of garlic, and a mixture of light olive and walnut oils. Serve alongside green salad leaves.

If you're after **MORE FIREPIT IDEAS**, look no further than a pork shoulder or two for cooking underground, each wrapped with a generous handful of woody herbs and chopped garlic. This will work almost as well in a slow oven, but the smoke from the pit sends it over the edge. Serve the sliced pork with a salsa verde and roasted beets, fennel and potatoes, or, my favorite, with a homemade apple sauce, peppered with chopped rosemary, and crusty white rolls.

If you make a roast, for however many, it's such a good idea to make a **GRAVY IN ADVANCE** and keep it in a pitcher in the refrigerator overnight. I fry onions, sprinkle them with flour, then gradually pour in some seriously good stock (use your very best) and a dash of wine. Whisk over medium heat for a good 5 minutes until thickened and smooth. Strain into a pitcher and set aside to cool. This way, all the stirring and simmering has been done the day before. While the meat rests, your gravy can be whisked into the de-fatted roasting pan—over the heat—to warm through and incorporate the flavors of the roast. Remember, you can never have too much gravy.

There's absolutely nothing wrong with turning out a crowd-pleaser. It's a rare Sunday luncher who doesn't love vanilla ice cream, or indeed custard, with **A RUSTIC CRUMBLE**. Apple, or apple and blackberry, frequently get top votes, so don't feel you have constantly to reinvent the wheel.

My mother incorporates crushed ratafia or amaretti cookies into a basic crumble recipe to great effect, and I suggest you do, too. Another of her tricks I always copy is to dot half-teaspoonfuls of brown sugar over the crumble surface and lay a tiny sliver of butter on each pile. The sugar and butter will melt into bubbling pools of toffee in the oven. As a kid, I would sneak to the refrigerator later and polish off the leftover toffee disks, blithely assuming nobody would notice their absence. They always did.

Crumble topping can be made in advance and kept frozen, ready to use as needed. The raw, assembled crumble will freeze well for a few months, too; bake from frozen.

INDEX